The Road to Love:
Zen Meditation Practice For Beginners

Roshi Tchogen & Ting Chen

With Foreword by Tenzin Gyatso
the 14th Dalai Lama

NMD Books
Simi Valley, CA

Copyright 2016 –Roshi Tchogen & Ting Chen
All rights reserved. No part of this book may be reproduced in any format or by any means without written permission from the publisher.

Library of Congress Cataloging-in-Publication
The Road to Love: Zen Meditation Practice For Beginners
Roshi Tchogen & Ting Chen
ISBN: 978-1-936828-47-0

First Edition March 2016

Contents

Foreword to the New Edition by the 14th Dalai Lama 4

Translator's Original Introduction 19

The Levels Of Buddhist Discipline 28

Preparing For Meditation 31

Regulating the Mind 41

Counting the Breath 75

Varieties of Ch'an 81

Recommended Postures 88

Meditation Styles and Techniques 92

Glossary of Zazen & Buddhist Terms 101

Foreword

By Tenzin Gyatso; The Fourteenth Dalai Lama

ONE GREAT QUESTION underlies our experience, whether we think about it consciously or not: What is the purpose of life? I have considered this question and would like to share my thoughts in the hope that they may be of direct, practical benefit to those who read them.

I believe that the purpose of life is to be happy. From the moment of birth, every human being wants happiness and does not want suffering. Neither social conditioning nor education nor ideology affect this. From the very core of our being, we simply desire contentment. I don't know whether the universe, with its countless galaxies, stars and planets, has a deeper meaning or not, but at the very least, it is clear that we humans who live on this earth face the task of making a happy life for ourselves. Therefore, it is important to discover what will bring about the greatest degree of happiness.

How to achieve happiness

For a start, it is possible to divide every kind of happiness and suffering into two main categories: mental and physical. Of the two, it is the mind that exerts the greatest influence on most of us. Unless we are either gravely ill or deprived of basic necessities, our physical condition plays a secondary role in life. If the body is content, we virtually ignore it. The mind, however, registers every event, no matter how small. Hence we should devote our most serious efforts to bringing about mental peace.

From my own limited experience I have found that the greatest degree of inner tranquility comes from the development of love and compassion.

The more we care for the happiness of others, the greater our own sense of well-being becomes. Cultivating a close, warm-hearted feeling for others automatically puts the mind at ease. This helps remove whatever fears or insecurities we may have and gives us the strength to cope with any obstacles we encounter. It is the ultimate source of success in life.

As long as we live in this world we are bound to encounter problems. If, at such times, we lose hope and become discouraged, we diminish our ability to face difficulties. If, on the other hand, we remember that it is not just ourselves but every one who has to undergo suffering, this more realistic perspective will increase our determination and capacity to overcome troubles. Indeed, with this attitude, each new obstacle can be seen as yet another valuable opportunity to improve our mind!

Thus we can strive gradually to become more compassionate, that is we can develop both genuine sympathy for others' suffering and the will to help remove their pain. As a result, our own serenity and inner strength will increase.

Our need for love

Ultimately, the reason why love and compassion bring the greatest happiness is simply that our nature cherishes them above all else. The need for love lies at the very foundation of human existence. It results from the profound interdependence we all share with one another. However capable and skillful an individual may be, left alone, he or she will not survive. However vigorous and independent one may feel during the most prosperous periods of life, when one is sick or very young or very old, one must depend on the support of others.

Inter-dependence, of course, is a fundamental law of nature. Not only higher forms of life but also many of the smallest insects are social beings who, without any religion, law or education, survive by mutual cooperation based on an innate recognition of their interconnectedness. The most subtle level of material phenomena is also governed by interdependence. All phenomena from the planet we inhabit to the oceans, clouds, forests and flowers that surround us, arise in dependence upon subtle patterns of energy. Without their proper interaction, they dissolve and decay.

It is because our own human existence is so dependent on the help of others that our need for love lies at the very foundation of our existence. Therefore we need a genuine sense of responsibility and a sincere concern for the welfare of others.

We have to consider what we human beings really are. We are not like machine-made objects. If we are merely mechanical entities, then machines themselves could alleviate all of our sufferings and fulfill our needs.

However, since we are not solely material creatures, it is a mistake to place all our hopes for happiness on external development alone. Instead, we should consider our origins and nature to discover what we require.

Leaving aside the complex question of the creation and evolution of our universe, we can at least agree that each of us is the product of our own parents. In general, our conception took place not just in the context of sexual desire but from our parents' decision to have a child. Such decisions are founded on responsibility and altruism — the parents compassionate commitment to care of their child until it is able to take care of itself. Thus, from the very moment of our conception, our parents' love is directly in our creation.

Moreover, we are completely dependent upon our mothers' care from the earliest stages of our growth. According to some scientists, a pregnant woman's mental state, be it calm or agitated, has a direct physical effect on her unborn child.

The expression of love is also very important at the time of birth. Since the very first thing we do is suck milk from our mothers' breast, we naturally feel close to her, and she must feel love for us in order to feed us properly; if she feels anger or resentment her milk may not flow freely.

Then there is the critical period of brain development from the time of birth up to at least the age of three or four, during which time loving physical contact is the single most important factor for the normal growth of the child. If the child is not held, hugged, cuddled, or loved, its development will be impaired and its brain will not mature properly.

Since a child cannot survive without the care of others, love is its most important nourishment. The happiness of childhood, the allaying of the child's many fears and the healthy development of its self-confidence all depend directly upon love.

Nowadays, many children grow up in unhappy homes. If they do not receive proper affection, in later life they will rarely love their parents and, not infrequently, will find it hard to love others. This is very sad.

As children grow older and enter school, their need for support must be met by their teachers. If a teacher not only imparts academic education but also assumes responsibility for preparing students for life, his or her pupils will feel trust and respect and what has been taught will leave an indelible impression on their minds. On the other hand, subjects taught by a teacher who does not show true concern for his or her students' overall well-being will be regarded as temporary and not retained for long.

Similarly, if one is sick and being treated in hospital by a doctor who evinces a warm human feeling, one feels at ease and the doctors' desire to give the best possible care is itself curative, irrespective of the degree of his or her technical skill. On the other hand, if one's doctor lacks human feeling and displays an unfriendly expression, impatience or casual disregard, one will feel anxious, even if he or she is the most highly qualified doctor and the disease has been correctly diagnosed and the right medication prescribed. Inevitably, patients' feelings make a difference to the quality and completeness of their recovery.

Even when we engage in ordinary conversation in everyday life, if someone speaks with human feeling we enjoy listening, and respond accordingly; the whole conversation becomes interesting, however unimportant the topic may be. On the other hand, if a person speaks coldly or harshly, we feel uneasy and wish for a quick end to the interaction. From the least to the most important event, the affection and respect of others are vital for our happiness.

Recently I met a group of scientists in America who said that the rate of mental illness in their country was quite high-around twelve percent of the population. It became clear during our discussion that the main cause of depression was not a lack of material necessities but a deprivation of the affection of the others.

So, as you can see from everything I have written so far, one thing seems clear to me: whether or not we are consciously aware of it, from the day we are born, the need for human affection is in our very blood. Even if the affection comes from an animal or someone we would normally consider an enemy, both children and adults will naturally gravitate towards it.

I believe that no one is born free from the need for love. And this demonstrates that, although some modern schools of thought seek to do so, human beings cannot be defined as solely physical. No material object, however beautiful or valuable, can make us feel loved, because our deeper identity and true character lie in the subjective nature of the mind.

Developing compassion

Some of my friends have told me that, while love and compassion are marvelous and good, they are not really very relevant. Our world, they say, is not a place where such beliefs have much influence or power. They claim that anger and hatred are so much a part of human nature that humanity will always be dominated by them. I do not agree.

We humans have existed in our present form for about a hundred-thousand years. I believe that if during this time the human mind had been primarily controlled by anger and hatred, our overall population would have decreased. But today, despite all our wars, we find that the human population is greater than ever. This clearly indicates to me that love and compassion predominate in the world. And this is why unpleasant events are news, compassionate activities are so much part of daily life that they are taken for granted and, therefore, largely ignored.

So far I have been discussing mainly the mental benefits of compassion, but it contributes to good physical health as well, According to my personal experience, mental stability and physical well-being are directly related. Without question, anger and agitation make us more susceptible to illness. On the other hand, if the mind is tranquil and occupied with positive thoughts, the body will not easily fall prey to disease.

But of course it is also true that we all have an innate self-centeredness that inhibits our love for others. So, since we desire the true happiness that is brought about by only a calm mind, and since such peace of mind is brought about by only a compassionate attitude, how can we develop this? Obviously, it is not enough for us simply to think about how nice compassion is! We need to make a concerted effort to develop it; we must use all the events of our daily life to transform our thoughts and behavior.

First of all, we must be clear about what we mean by compassion. Many forms of compassionate feeling are mixed with desire and attachment. For instance, the love parents feel of their child is often strongly associated with their own emotional needs, so it is not fully compassionate. Again, in marriage, the love between husband and wife — particularly at the beginning, when each partner still may not know the other's deeper character very well — depends more on attachment than genuine love. Our desire can be so strong that the person to whom we are attached appears to be good, when in fact he or she is very negative. In addition, we have a tendency to exaggerate small positive qualities. Thus when one partner's attitude changes, the other partner is often disappointed and his or her attitude changes too. This is an indication that love has been motivated more by personal need than by genuine care for the other individual.

True compassion is not just an emotional response but a firm commitment founded on reason. Therefore, a truly compassionate attitude towards others does not change even if they behave negatively.

Of course, developing this kind of compassion is not at all easy! As a start, let us consider the following facts:

Whether people are beautiful and friendly or unattractive and disruptive, ultimately they are human beings, just like oneself. Like oneself, they want happiness and do not want suffering. Furthermore, their right to overcome suffering and be happy is equal to one's own. Now, when you recognize that all beings are equal in both their desire for happiness and their right to obtain it, you automatically feel empathy and closeness for them. Through accustoming your mind to this sense of universal altruism, you develop a feeling of responsibility for others: the wish to help them actively overcome their problems. Nor is this wish selective; it applies equally to all. As long as they are human beings experiencing pleasure and pain just as you do, there is no logical basis to discriminate between them or to alter your concern for them if they behave negatively.

Let me emphasize that it is within your power, given patience and time, to develop this kind of compassion. Of course, our self-centeredness, our distinctive attachment to the feeling of an independent, self-existent entity, works fundamentally to inhibit our compassion. Indeed, true compassion can be experienced only when this type of self- grasping is eliminated. But this does not mean that we cannot start and make progress now.

How can we start

We should begin by removing the greatest hindrances to compassion: anger and hatred. As we all know, these are extremely powerful emotions and they can overwhelm our entire mind. Nevertheless, they can be controlled. If, however, they are not, these negative emotions will plague us — with no extra effort on their part! — and impede our quest for the happiness of a loving mind.

So as a start, it is useful to investigate whether or not anger is of value. Sometimes, when we are discouraged by a difficult situation, anger does seem helpful, appearing to bring with it more energy, confidence and determination.

Here, though, we must examine our mental state carefully. While itis true that anger brings extra energy, if we explore the nature of this energy, we discover that it is blind: we cannot be sure whether its result will be positive or negative. This is because anger eclipses the best part of our brain: its rationality. So the energy of anger is almost always unreliable. It can cause an immense amount of destructive, unfortunate behavior. Moreover, if anger increases to the extreme, one becomes like a mad person, acting in ways that are as damaging to oneself as they are to others.

It is possible, however, to develop an equally forceful but far more controlled energy with which to handle difficult situations.

This controlled energy comes not only from a compassionate attitude, but also from reason and patience. These are the most powerful antidotes to anger. Unfortunately, many people misjudge these qualities as signs of weakness. I believe the opposite to be true: that they are the true signs of inner strength. Compassion is by nature gentle, peaceful and soft, but it is very powerful. It is those who easily lose their patience who are insecure and unstable. Thus, to me, the arousal of anger is a direct sign of weakness.

So, when a problem first arises, try to remain humble and maintain a sincere attitude and be concerned that the outcome is fair. Of course, others may try to take advantage of you, and if your remaining detached only encourages unjust aggression, adopt a strong stand, This, however, should be done with compassion, and if it is necessary to express your views and take strong countermeasures, do so without anger or ill-intent.

You should realize that even though your opponents appear to be harming you, in the end, their destructive activity will damage only themselves. In order to check your own selfish impulse to retaliate, you should recall your desire to practice compassion and assume responsibility for helping prevent the other person from suffering the consequences of his or her acts.

Thus, because the measures you employ have been calmly chosen, they will be more effective, more accurate and more forceful. Retaliation based on the blind energy of anger seldom hits the target.

Friends and enemies

I must emphasize again that merely thinking that compassion and reason and patience are good will not be enough to develop them. We must wait for difficulties to arise and then attempt to practice them.

And who creates such opportunities? Not our friends, of course, but our enemies. They are the ones who give us the most trouble, So if we truly wish to learn, we should consider enemies to be our best teacher!

For a person who cherishes compassion and love, the practice of tolerance is essential, and for that, an enemy is indispensable. So we should feel grateful to our enemies, for it is they who can best help us develop a tranquil mind! Also, itis often the case in both personal and public life, that with a change in circumstances, enemies become friends.

So anger and hatred are always harmful, and unless we train our minds and work to reduce their negative force, they will continue to disturb us and disrupt our attempts to develop a calm mind. Anger and hatred are our real enemies. These are the forces we most need to confront and defeat, not the temporary enemies who appear intermittently throughout life.

Of course, it is natural and right that we all want friends. I often joke that if you really want to be selfish, you should be very altruistic! You should take good care of others, be concerned for their welfare, help them, serve them, make more friends, make more smiles. The result? When you yourself need help, you find plenty of helpers! If, on the other hand, you neglect the happiness of others, in the long term you will be the loser. And is friendship produced through quarrels and anger, jealousy and intense competitiveness? I do not think so. Only affection brings us genuine close friends.

In today's materialistic society, if you have money and power, you seem to have many friends. But they are not friends of yours; they are the friends of your money and power. When you lose your wealth and influence, you will find it very difficult to track these people down.

The trouble is that when things in the world go well for us, we become confident that we can manage by ourselves and feel we do not need friends, but as our status and health decline, we quickly realize how wrong we were. That is the moment when we learn who is really helpful and who is completely useless. So to prepare for that moment, to make genuine friends who will help us when the need arises, we ourselves must cultivate altruism!

Though sometimes people laugh when I say it, I myself always want more friends. I love smiles. Because of this I have the problem of knowing how to make more friends and how to get more smiles, in particular, genuine smiles. For there are many kinds of smile, such as sarcastic, artificial or diplomatic smiles. Many smiles produce no feeling of satisfaction, and sometimes they can even create suspicion or fear, can't they? But a genuine smile really gives us a feeling of freshness and is, I believe, unique to human beings. If these are the smiles we want, then we ourselves must create the reasons for them to appear.

Compassion and the world

In conclusion, I would like briefly to expand my thoughts beyond the topic of this short piece and make a wider point: individual happiness can contribute in a profound and effective way to the overall improvement of our entire human community.

Because we all share an identical need for love, it is possible to feel that anybody we meet, in whatever circumstances, is a brother or sister. No matter how new the face or how different the dress and behavior, there is no significant division between us and other people. It is foolish to dwell on external differences, because our basic natures are the same.

Ultimately, humanity is one and this small planet is our only home, If we are to protect this home of ours, each of us needs to experience a vivid sense of universal altruism. It is only this feeling that can remove the self-centered motives that cause people to deceive and misuse one another.

If you have a sincere and open heart, you naturally feel self-worth and confidence, and there is no need to be fearful of others.

I believe that at every level of society — familial, tribal, national and international — the key to a happier and more successful world is the growth of compassion. We do not need to become religious, nor do we need to believe in an ideology. All that is necessary is for each of us to develop our good human qualities.

I try to treat whoever I meet as an old friend. This gives me a genuine feeling of happiness. It is the practice of compassion.

Translator's Original Introduction

Originally, one's own mind and nature are pure, and there is nothing to accept and nothing to refuse; there is neither existence nor non-existence; there is only clear understanding without attachment and with no dwelling. One who wants to know the non-attachment, non-dwelling mind can find it through meditation, because it is only then that the mind does not think of right and wrong, of good and evil or of self and others.

If this seems obscure, then consider the following: The past is already gone; when you do not think of it, the thought of the past is gone, too. Then, there is no past nor any thought of the past. Furthermore, the future has yet not arrived. If you do not wish for nor seek after it, the thought regarding the future vanishes. Then, there is no future nor any thought about the future. Finally, the present is already present. Without grasping at it or dwelling upon it and without there being any thought about it, the thought of the present disappears, and there is no present nor any thought of the present. The mind that does not dwell on anything whatsoever is known as the True Mind or Original Nature.

The non-dwelling mind is the mind of the Buddha, it is the mind of liberation, it is the mind of Bodhi, and it is the mind of non-birth. So, if you really want meditation to come about, sit properly erect and close your eyes. Then purify your mind, lay down everything and think of neither good nor evil. Just observe your thoughts. As you look for their place of origin, you discover that they suddenly rise up and just as suddenly disappear, and that this process goes on and on. Be patient and continue to observe them, and you will, in time, know the thoughts to be devoid of any self-nature; also you will, thereby, know original emptiness. Do not attempt to follow the thoughts, to trace them in any way or have any intention of getting rid of them, and, in time, awareness will manifest as your mind illumines a thought. Then, there will suddenly be a stillness that becomes suchness. At some point, another thought will arise, and you will observe it in the same way.

Do this at least once a day, sitting from fifteen minutes to an hour. As your concentration deepens, your thoughts slow down and diminish in number, and your power of illumination increases until you eventually find out that not a single thought arises. Then, there is only stillness and voidness, for then the mind is clear and pure. This is your self-nature as known directly through wisdom (Prajna).

The subject of wisdom is Prajna, and the opposite of Prajna is ignorance. Prajna illuminates the delusion that is ignorance. With continued exposure to Prajna, ignorance wears away bit by bit until there is a return to self-nature, or pure mind. It is in this situation that Right Thought manifests. There is no longer the duality of subject/object. This state is also known as no-thought or suchness and is also referred to as the inconceivable. When the mind is illumined and a thought, as one ordinarily knows it to be, arises, it dissolves instantly. Continue to practice in this way on a daily basis, and you will notice your self-nature getting steadily clearer and purer. Then there will be no longer any need to observe, nor will there be any purpose to observe. Indeed, there will be no longer any need of any kind. It will be realized that mind is no-mind, that no-mind is pure mind and that pure mind is the true mind. At that time, the sound of discussion and the role of thought will be finished. It cannot be expressed in words, and yet it is as simple as drinking water and knowing whether it is cold or warm. It is called Sudden Enlightenment.

It is my express wish that this guide, based on the meditation manual of Ting Chen, will prove helpful in imparting the Dharma to its readers. In helping me reach this goal, I wish to thank Sam Langberg and Dr. Frank G. French, without whose help regarding fine points in the translation and without whose editorial acuteness this task might have proved too difficult. May this work, then, help everyone to generate the Bodhi Mind and never to regress.

Why Meditate?

When you are caught up in the emotional upheaval of greed, anger and delusion, you may find yourself succumbing to some very real physical ailments; and when you are ill, the world may seem to be a very dismal place. That is not to say, however, that all of our illnesses are due to extreme emotions. Exposure to substances to which you may be allergic can alter everything about you. It can cause violent mood swings, depression, hallucinations and all sorts of physical effects, including actual tissue damage. Whatever the cause, disease is most often accompanied by an assortment of disruptive emotions. Programs that have been designed to make therapeutic use of relaxation methods and meditation have proved to be effective in curbing both the physical effects and the emotions which accompany them. Yet, as beneficial as they may be, such methods can take one only so far.

In the Buddhist tradition, meditation is used to defuse the source of all the trouble the illusion of self and other. In Ch'an (or Zen), the aim is to overcome thought and defilement. Having done this, and with thoughts no longer stirring, the real substance of mind becomes evident. Without thoughts and without the illusion of self and other, greed, anger and hatred have no place to arise; and the energy that was tied up by those illusions becomes available, helping to provide an overall improvement in health. That is why meditation is called The Fundamental Practice.

The Psychophysiological Effects of Meditation

The Russian physiologist, Ivan Pavlov (18491936), emphasized the role that the cerebrum plays in physiology. At first glance, one might assume this to be merely a statement of fact, because that part of the brain is usually thought to involve little else other than thinking. Actually, it takes part in the production of many hormones, both directly and indirectly. Every aspect of a person is interrelated, and that is how and why thoughts and emotions can have such far-reaching effects. That is, however, also why meditation and calm-inducing thoughts can become so stabilizing and so healthy. One can safely assume, then, that most of what contributes to proper functioning also contributes to good health.

Useful Hints for Better Practice and Better Health

As you progress in your practice, you are required to sit motionless for longer and longer periods of time at a stretch. It is then that some very important physical limitations may oblige you to make some adjustments in the way that you sit. Should you choose to ignore them, thinking that there is just one right way to practice, you may cause yourself needless pain and distraction (which means that you will not be able to concentrate); and you may possibly expose yourself to irreparable physical damage as well.

It is not unusual for people who have gone on retreats to return with painfully damaged knees, having held a position in spite of pain and having welcomed an ensuing numbness, simply because they have more trouble than they can remedy. To paraphrase **The Kalama Sutra**, "Do not do something because you have been instructed to do so, but try it and find out how it works for you." Be always on guard for what doesn't seem to be quite right, and see what might be done about it. There are many, many methods that can be tried. There is no reason to have to submit to pain or outright debility, especially when nothing good can come of it.

The Relationship Between Mind And Meditation

The metaphor of the mirror, often referred to in Ch'an, is most suitable here in pointing out the most salient aspects of meditation as practiced in this tradition. The mirror mind does not respond at all, and it is by this lack of agitation that all things are clearly known. This is how the mind is said to be when there is no clinging. The mind, to be like a mirror, must be passive, detached, uninterested and quiet. It is a time of rest, recuperation and of learning to be undefiled in the midst of what is normally defiling. When there is no perturbation in the mind, just as when there are no ripples on the surface of a lake, all things are mirrored clearly, leaving no trace. There are no intentions, and there is no action to be taken or not taken. There is no dependence upon anything that you do or do not do. Meditation just unfolds naturally as the mind grows tranquil.

Concentration

If you make the sun's rays converge, using a magnifying glass, and focus the resulting point of light onto a sheet of paper, you can easily burn a hole through it. Similarly, when you concentrate your thoughts, you are empowered in many ways. A lay Buddhist, Yang Jen San, once found a copy of **The Surangama Sutra** in an old bookstore. He was overjoyed. It was just what he had been looking for. He sat down and read and read in complete absorption, oblivious to his surroundings, until someone called him. Suddenly he noticed it had become dark and that if he wanted to continue, he would have to light a lamp. Wondrous things must happen in deep concentration, for he had been reading in the dark! A very famous writer of the Sung Dynasty, Su Dong Pu, recounted a similar experience in which he was so deeply engrossed in painting a picture that he was no longer aware of his person nor of anything else. It is as though where wholehearted application is directed, the whole world must step aside.

Wellbeing and ease ensues. Sustained, relaxed concentration of this type easily becomes meditation. Unfolding naturally, if allowed to continue, it improves one's health and vitality, as stultified emotions and their physical concomitants give way to healing. The health-enhancing benefits of meditation are now a matter of record, and numerous physicians include it in programs for their patients' recoveries.

The average person's mind is in turmoil. He or she is the product of deeprooted patterns of thought resulting from karma accumulated since time immemorial, as well as being tortured by the illusion of self. To be enlightened is to be free of all of that. Concentration already reduces the turmoil by limiting one's attention to just one thing. Through this practice, the apparent hold that you have on your illusion of self and things gives way until there is meditation. Then, there is an absence of thought and an absence of words. Then, without the stress and the strain of delusion, a very deep sort of healing takes place.

Meditation and Dhyana

In Buddhism, the ordinary man is seen as leading a life steeped in suffering through the defilements of greed, anger and delusion. It is only when he finds out, firsthand, that there is, indeed, nothing that he does that is free of defilement and suffering and that there is a way out of it all, that he may become sufficiently well-motivated to gain that freedom. This is traditionally likened to the discovery that the pretty, colored rope that one has found and treasures is actually a very poisonous snake. When that is your experience, you may have such a profound understanding of Buddha-dharma that your life will turn around radically. You may realize beyond all doubt that, though the body may be strong and healthy, it still changes and grows old. You may realize deeply, by breaking off attachment to both body and mind, that birth, death, and defilement also no longer exist. In the Ch'an tradition, this is discovered through meditation.

Discipline (*sila*), and wisdom (*prajna*) are closely related to meditation (*dhyana*). Proper discipline leads to *dhyana*, and *dhyana* gives rise to *wisdom*. It is by means of discipline that the defilements are dispelled, and this eases the way for the cultivation of *dhyana* (established in the same region as *prajna*). The great *Ch'an Ting* (Chinese for *dhyana*-related meditative practice) is said to be secluded from defilement and suffering as the result of selfdiscipline. To free oneself from defilements is the main purpose of the practice of pure discipline. By means of discipline, defilements are dispelled. Then, *dhyana* can become established; defined variously as voidness, the absence of subject and object, *Ch'an Ting*, or that which is not of the flow of suffering, it is the access route to wisdom (*prajna*).

The Levels Of Buddhist Discipline

Also Known as Cumulative Discipline

Formally stated, the sevenfold assembly consists of the *upasaka* (male lay devotee), *upasika* (female lay devotee) *siksamana* (female candidate for novitiate), *sramanera* (novice monk), *sramanerika* (novice nun), (fully ordained monk), and *bhikhuni* (fully ordained nun). These terms designate levels of commitment to practice, starting with the basic five precepts, or training rules, for laity.

Not formally stated, but of equal importance, is the vow to do good and refrain from doing evil. One's actions should always be for the benefit of all sentient beings. The thrust of Buddhist discipline is a blameless coexistence with the rest of the world, as well as improved mindfulness and inner peace. There are two ways to uphold the precepts. One is called *stop and hold*, which means that one should stop, or refrain from doing evil, and *hold* to the precepts. The second one is called *to do and to hold*. This simply means that you should do good and abide by the discipline. The discipline has the function of helping you avoid evil and do good, and upholding it enables you to purify your body and mind. While that is being accomplished, the outflow of impurities, or *asrava*, diminishes; and these conditions, in turn, facilitate *samadhi*.

Dhyana is absorption meditation at varying levels; when extended over long periods of time, it is sometimes referred to as samadhi. These levels (usually four) are accounted for in Ch'an practice, and there are, as well, several different kinds of Ch'an. There are, for example, mundane Ch'an, supramundane Ch'an, and the Ch'an of the highest Mahayana realization, to mention only three.

Meditation can be practiced while sitting, standing, walking or lying down and anywhere in between; but because our minds are ordinarily so very disorganized, the best way to practice for most of us is to sit regularly in a quiet place. Having seated yourself, simply put everything else aside and concentrate on whatever your object of concentration may be. With your mind, speech and action already cooled down through discipline, there is occasion for natural and steady access to *samadhi*. When no thought arises, the pure substance of mind appears; and the state of stillness and illumination gradually manifests itself.

The quality of that stillness is undefinable, and yet it is not as if the sitter were a statue carved from stone. In this context, *illumination* is understood as awareness without subject-object duality. There is no longer someone being aware of *something*, and, consequently, there is no need for thought or verbalization.

The early sages emphasized that a moment of meditation honors Buddha more than building pagodas as numerous as the sandgrains in the Ganges River. The pagodas, it is argued, can be demolished, unlike the onepointed mind that transcends time and space.

It cannot be repeated often enough that very little can be achieved without observing the precepts. Indeed, discipline dispels the attachment and the suffering that accompany it and leads to the passionless, pure path to

Nirvana. *Anasrava*, or passionless purity, is the opposite of asrava, the outflow of the passions and their filth. *Asrava* is further known as the discharge of mindenergy leading to the loss of truth. *Anasrava*, by definition, means the absence of outflow and seclusion from the stream of passion and, thus, from the stream of suffering.

Preparing For Meditation

The Posture

Find an uncluttered, well-ventilated (non-drafty), quiet place where you can sit undisturbed on a regular schedule. You may use a cover to protect yourself from the cold.

In the beginning, let comfort be your guide. Make sure you set up a schedule you can live with, and then keep to it faithfully. Adjust your sittings so that there is no excess of discomfort or pain, which includes finding a posture you can hold for a period of time that you will gradually extend. Learn to relax completely; do not try to control anything, and don't expect anything.

Make sure the garments you wear are comfortable and loose, and wear as few of them as circumstances permit. Loosen your belt or whatever might be binding or distracting, such as a wristwatch, jewelry or scent. There is actually no need for adornments, and their use during meditation should be avoided.

The Legs

If, and only if, you can manage it, sit on the full lotus, which is the traditional position considered most stable. For those who might want to try the full lotus position, do as follows. First, sit on the floor or a low cushion and fold your right leg in front of you, pulling it in close to your groin. Next, fold your left leg over it, with your left foot resting, sole upward, on your right thigh and close to your groin. Finally, lift your right foot, sole up, onto your left thigh, bringing it in close to your groin. You may be able to maintain this position for a short time at first, but, as you grow accustomed to it, you may find it contributing greatly to a sense of quiet, tranquility and stability.

Sitting in the half-lotus position does not provide as firm a base because only one knee is weighted down by the opposite leg. To compensate for this, switch the position of your legs, if you can, with each sitting. If you find that this proves too difficult to do immediately, set aside time to gently lengthen the muscles of your legs, hips and groin; but beware that you don't pull a muscle or injure yourself in your eagerness, or you may have to take weeks to recuperate. Gradual, steady practice is advised and works for most people if they are loving, understanding and patient with themselves and, above all, if they are relaxed. Do not ever force yourself into a position or hold it when it brings on intense pain. It is not uncommon for misalignments to develop by twisting at the waist in order to have both knees touch the floor.

An effective way to help loosen the muscles that keep your legs from settling down on either side of you, so that they easily rest on the floor, can be done while sitting in a meditation seat. Sit on the very edge of your meditation seat with your feet placed shoulder-width apart and with your knees positioned directly over your ankles. Then lift one leg and rest the ankle of that leg on the thigh of the other, allowing the knee of the raised leg to descend out to the side as far as it can comfortably go, supporting it with your hands and then lifting it and lowering it over and over again. Each time you lower it, think that leg is relaxing more. Then set it again, and let go even more, trying to feel what may be necessary to have this happen. Be sure your hips remain level the whole time and that your legs sink lower and lower on either side. Be aware of and be mindful of everything that is happening in terms of your thoughts and deeds during this simple exercise. If, after your efforts, you cannot manage to sit comfortably in the full or the half lotus position, then you may wish to try the "free" position.

Should pain develop, stay with it for a while. Observe it, rather than lamenting your lot or wishing you were elsewhere, squirming, trying to escape or braving it out while gritting your teeth. Staying with your pain, you will soon clearly see how to succeed in your effort by the way you sit, the way you breathe and/or by the way you view the situation.

Borrowing from another source, we can take this advice: "Be still and know." Whatever comes, allow it to happen. Do not avoid or reject, but take in whatever is happening, including your way of coping. Even if your reaction is to get out of the situation, providing you become fully aware of what is happening, you are no longer so thoroughly caught up in it. Be mindful of what is happening in the present, for only *you* are in touch with the events, their causes and conditions.

It may be beneficial for you to explore your response when sending loving-kindness to yourself. It may feel embarrassing, silly or unbecoming; you may even find yourself inexplicably crying. As practiced in the Theravada tradition, in combination with *vipasyana*, the meditation on loving-kindness is simple and profound, yet very effective, in reaching the sources of our deep suffering. It is Dharma at its purest, inasmuch as it addresses compassion as well as being intimate with pain. Do you experience pain as if it were an *object* outside of you, an intruder? This approach can generate meaningful insights into the workings of your mind and should be explored.

However, you should let discretion be your guide. Do not submit to pain for the sake of absolving yourself of a sense of guilt or to prove how well-intentioned or how willing you are to endure torture. Consider it, rather, to be an act of loving-kindness or as mindfulness practice. Either way, it is expedient. However, if you find the pain too distracting, stretch out your legs mindfully, take a rest and return to sitting. If you can simply sit and not be involved in *sitting correctly* in order to achieve something, you will find yourself becoming increasingly quiet, your breath becoming more subtle and your muscles becoming more relaxed; then meditation ensues quite naturally.

Chest, Abdomen, Buttocks

Raise your chest a little, moving it forward, and sit so that the hollow part of your chest, the part that is at about the level of the base of your sternum (the den of your heart), permits your diaphragm to function unimpeded. Newcomers to meditation often experience obstruction and discomfort in the chest, and that is usually caused by the den of the heart not being low enough. Should that occur, focus your awareness on your abdomen and refrain from any effort; you should feel relief in a short time. Your buttocks should be protruding a little, and your back should be comfortably, easily erect. Sit relaxed and self=composed, settling into your lower abdomen. This practice has been found to be especially calming.

Hands

Sitting in the half-lotus position, make sure your right foot is on top of your left thigh. Your palms are turned up, with the back of your right hand resting in the palm of your left, while the back of your left hand rests at about the level of your *tant'ien* (or the lower part of your abdomen).

n the full-lotus position, the legs are crossed a little above the ankles, with the left leg uppermost. Here, the back of your left hand is cradled at the place where your legs cross.

When these positions become natural and comfortable, there is usually an accompanying sense of ease, silence and tranquility.

Natural Breathing

The abdomen relaxes and expands as you inhale and contracts as you exhale. This is, indeed, natural; for when you exhale, the diaphragm moves upward into the chest, while the abdomen simultaneously contracts. The contraction not only assists in evacuating the lungs, but also stimulates blood circulating through the organs contained in the abdominal cavity by compressing the viscera.

Right Breathing

The abdomen is contracted as you inhale, and it relaxes as you exhale. This sort of breathing has been used in China since ancient times as a kind of physical and mental hygiene. Try both methods to discover whatever advantages each seems to hold for you, the practitioner, lest you get caught up in having to have things happen in only a certain way.

Breathing Practice

While you are relaxed, it becomes profoundly evident that breathing simply goes on and that there is the knowing that it does. You can intentionally breathe in a certain way, but the need for doing so is based upon some external circumstances bringing about the need for the intention, so that the matter of choice seems somewhat obviated; thus, intention seems to come about almost capriciously, in spite of yourself, as it were. This paradox exists in everything that we do. Meditation takes place in the absence of thought, and yet we think that without thought there can be no meditation. Perhaps the answer to this conundrum lies in the sequence of two separate events rather than in what seems their apparent opposition. For example, when you are actively paying attention to your breath, you cannot be calm; and so you are advised simply to relax so calm can ensue. Meditation is distinguished by absence of thought and a very characteristic sort of breathing, neither of which can be brought about at will. Control must first be relinquished. You circuitously bring that about by applying whatever you may have discovered about relaxation, and that is the full extent of exerting your will. The following rule holds true, whether you practice natural breathing or right breathing: *When you sit down to meditate, sit easily erect, breathing through your nose.*

At first, your breathing may be rapid and shallow. As you relax and have the attitude of neither accepting nor rejecting whatever arises, your breathing slows down and deepens until you find that you inhale and exhale, in a cycle, once every minute. Ease may be conceived of as the standard. At no time should anything feel forced or uncomfortable; rather, it should all just happen free of any concern on your part.

As you continue to sit, your breath grows finer and finer. You should devote, at the very least, five minutes each morning and each evening to this breathing relaxation practice. Practice as often as you can during the rest of the day, wherever and whenever you happen to think of it. As the breath slows and becomes increasingly subtle, the mind stabilizes and grows calm. As the mind goes, so goes the breath. To illustrate this, four kinds of breath are noted as evolving in the course of practice:

The first is called *windy breath* to describe the sound that you make as you breathe.

The second is known as *gasping breath*. Here, you no longer make any sound when you breathe but have the feeling that you cannot inhale enough.

In the third type of breathing, the breath is even and silent and without any obstruction, but you have yet to feel calm. This is called *air breath*. These first three ways of breathing are still roughhewn and still show signs of unrest.

When there is neither sound nor obstruction, neither roughness nor softness, and in that very quiet time when you do not feel that you are breathing at all and breathing evokes no association of any kind, you have achieved the fourth kind of breath, *silent breath*.

It is the breath that harmonizes. If you find that you easily grow calm and that your breath quickly becomes fine, this indicates that your mind is easily stabilized. With continued practice, it may take only a few moments for your breath to be regulated, and then the need to breathe will diminish and vanish; and, with that, you will no longer be disturbed by anything. Your mind, at this stage, is said to be quiet and stable. On the way to this trouble-free state, however, there is bound to be much discomfort and restlessness. If this persists, and to help to harmonize the breath, you can try the following methods, progressing from one to the next as you grow proficient. Very relaxedly and unconcernedly count from 1 to 10 in all of these exercises:

Count your breaths, calling one exhalation and inhalation just one breath;

Count only your inhalations;

Count only your exhalations.

When you have reached ten, resume counting from number one. Gradually, as your skill develops, you will be able to count to one hundred in ten groups of ten, without having your mind wander and without dropping off to sleep. However, should that happen, you are required to return to one and start all over again. As you grow more at ease, your mind and breath will, slowly and peacefully, become interdependent. Confusion and sleepiness decrease in all three breathing methods of concentration, and the mind is calmed as well.

When the goals of breath-counting have been reached, your next step will be to trace your breath. The mind, by this time, will be very calm and very concentrated. By tracing your breath, this calm and this concentration deepen until the breath is felt to enter and leave through all of your pores. As you continue in this way, you will come to experience yourself *dissipating like a cloud and melting away like a fog*, until there is nothing but voidness. When this happens, you find yourself freed of all sorts of illness, as the mind is established on a new, deeper level of quiet; and it is then that it is time to dispense with the method of tracing the breath.

Regulating the Mind

Meditation can improve your health, but its primary purpose is to enable you to be free of thought; because when this has occurred, wisdom shines brightly. With that aim in mind, then, we see that both *counting the breath and tracing the breath* are methods of regulating the breath and thereby the mind. If you are fully concentrated in this way, your thoughts are no longer confused or disordered. That is why people who have racing minds or who are involved in emotional turmoil are assigned the simple task of counting their breaths. It calms them in body, breath and mind. In body, they grow relaxed and free of tension, the breathing slows and deepens, and the mind grows quiet, calm and unperturbed.

As one continues in this practice, all but the finer states of mind disappear. Then, it is time to regulate the mind, for now it has become much less erratic. There are many methods of approach, but the one most favored is to have one rest his or her attention on just one point, and to consider any thoughts that arise to be like actors that appear on a stage and then leave. This attitude of passivity, of taking part less and less in what is happening, leads to concentration. Therefore, when you have succeeded in concentrating on the point of your choice, you are also free of disturbing thoughts; and, with continued concentration, the practitioner finds, as well, that fewer disturbing thoughts arise for the rest of the day. So, concentrate upon or relaxedly be aware of the tip of your nose, your navel or the point an inch and a half below it, in an area known as the *tan t'ien*, because your mind needs something to occupy it. Traditionally, in this practice the mind is said to be like a monkey that has been restricted to a small space, where it can no longer jump and skip about.

Two things plague you most when you are preparing the ground, as it were, from which meditation sprouts:

When you first sit down, your mind is restless and unstable. You are pulled in all directions, eager to succeed one moment and frustrated when things don't turn out the way you want the next. You may begin to ache, first in one place and then in another, so that all of your time is taken up trying to escape the pain or consoling yourself, or both. You may imagine yourself elsewhere, participating in events that have taken place in your life, or that events that are somehow important to you are taking place again. You may find yourself dozing off over and over again.

Through continuing practice, your mind becomes more settled, and discriminating thought diminishes; but there is still confusion, and you easily tire and doze off. It is to deal with these problems that you should sense the point an inch and a half below your navel and about an inch and a half in, which is in the area called the *tan t'ien*. This will not only correct your disordered thought and keep you from drifting off in reverie, but it also has a recognized physiologically stabilizing effect that results in mental and physical health as well. Again, you have to find the point to concentrate on that works for you. It might be the tip of your nose, your navel or the point an inch and a half below it. Whatever you choose to do, however, stay with it for the duration of the time that you have set aside for sitting. Beginners, especially, should make their practice more successful by finding the time to meditate when they are most alert, by eliminating discomfort and distraction and, most of all, by understanding the purpose of it all.

Insight Meditation

The method of concentration described thus far, in which you are to return to your object of concentration when you discover that you are caught up in discriminating thought, is a shallow way to grow calm and to stop wandering thoughts, because it involves thinking about the thoughts that arise, which is like adding fuel to a fire. It is not really a means of reaching calm, then, and so you must eventually abandon that method and take one more step to *insight meditation*. Ordinarily, you use your eyes to look *outside*. In this approach, you must literally put aside everything; close your eyes and observe and/or feel your discriminating thoughts. If you do, you will soon find you cannot hold onto them, dissolve them or send them away. Once this is deeply realized and you no longer struggle to hold onto them, dissolve them or send them away, you will know *original stillness* and *emptiness*. When this insight develops and you reflect in this way on a thought that arises, it quickly disappears and is replaced by voidness. This marks the creation of a radically new way in which the mind can work.

When you first set out to meditate, it may seem that your thought has lessened. After you have practiced for awhile, however, you will most likely feel that it has increased. What has actually increased is the realization of what has really been so right along, and this immediate and continuous source of suffering can serve as a lighthouse in the treacherous waters of *samsara*. This can be compared to not being aware of the dust rising in a room until a shaft of sunlight shines on it. In the same way, then, if you feel that you have too much thought, it is the first step toward enlightenment. Abandoning thought, persevering in the insight that permits this and delighting in this, usually over a long period of time, lead to a natural disappearance of thought. There is, instead, stillness. As you continue in this way, the stillness becomes more profound, for it becomes a stillness in which *sudden enlightenment* can occur.

Reciting the Name of Amitabha Buddha

As you may have realized, it is not unusual for thoughts to assail you relentlessly when you sit down to practice. Usually it is beyond your control, and, even with the best of intentions, one might eventually feel that there is no way to begin to practice. If you find that is more the rule than not for you, you might try the Pure Land approach, which is simply to recite the name of *Amitabha Buddha* over and over again. It is a very simple practice and can be very effective, but it requires a deep faith and a strong vow to be able to carry it out. However, if you sincerely recite the name of *Amitabha*, so that there is no other thought in your mind, and do this for some time, *false thought* will diminish.

Ch'an Master CheWu said that when a pure pearl is put into turbid water, the turbid water becomes pure. Similarly, when Buddha's name is put into a confused mind, that mind becomes Buddha. Ideally, reciting

Amitabha Buddha should free you of defilements in this very lifetime and assure your rebirth in the Pure Land as a great, bright light in the Ocean of Suffering, meriting praise for the Mahayana sutras and all the patriarchs and Dharma Masters of the past. Should you have any reservations about this practice, it must be said that this simple act of reciting *Amitabha* is profoundly Buddhist, because it engages body, speech and mind in one concerted effort the body by regulating the breath; the speech by confining it to a simple utterance; and the mind by a resolve which has been made and a vow which has been taken.

There are variations on this theme, as it were. You can recite aloud. You can recite silently. You can recite as you inhale. You can recite as you exhale. You can recite on both inhaling and exhaling. The rate at which you practice varies according to your particular needs and abilities, but this is true of any practice that you might engage in. The recitation should, in any event, proceed with the tranquility that comes from mind and breath depending on one another. As you continue in this way, the mind grows calm and the breath becomes shapeless. Then, it is as though only your original intention or vow functions, the recitation continuing on its own without disturbance or confusion until first the stage of *no-mind* is reached and then that of *no no-mind* is attained.

In **The Sutra of Ch'an Samadhi** it says that if a Bodhisattva meditates with nothing but the Buddha in mind, he obtains samadhi. This simple method of reciting the Buddha's name can rid you of discriminating thought, which is the *false thought* or the *thinking* that the common man is plagued with, and reward you with *Right Wisdom*; and because your breath is regulated, your health is improved too.

It might help you to count your recitations. Again, you can experiment to find out what works best for you. Count with each cycle of breathing in and out, preceding or following an exhalation; or just include it as part of each recitation. The count, here, can be anything that you decide upon, or you can simply continue to count from 1 to 10, as before, repeating it over and over. Or, again, you might even silently repeat your recitation ten times with each breath or as many times as you can. Any of the above approaches can help to bring about effective concentration, the object of them all being to provide you with something simple and repetitious to fully occupy your mind without disturbing it. You have to try it! You have to experiment with it! That is to say, now that you know the way to prepare a delicious and nutritious meal, you have to actually prepare it, taste it, see whether it agrees with you, improve on it, if need be, and then eat it until your health improves. By analogy you must use this procedure in your practice until the practice proceeds on its own and becomes, therefore, no longer practice but an art that seemingly has a life of its own.

During the T'ang Dynasty, Master FeiHsi composed a sastra on **The Reciting Buddha's Name Samadhi Sutra**. In it, he said that people use rare jade, crystal, diamonds or other precious things to make beads to use in meditation but that he himself traces his inhalations and exhalations (as they use beads) while reciting Amitabha and that, furthermore, he can do it while standing, sitting, lying down and even while in deep slumber.

What To Be Mindful Of

Every moment of every day presents an opportunity for meditation. However, you may feel that you are too busy or that you need a structure. In that case, you might try it upon arising in the morning and/or just before retiring at night. If you can make the attempt only once a day, experiment to find out what the best time for you is, not only in regard to availability but also in regard to the time when you feel most alert and responsive to practice. Look for quality in the short time set aside. In the beginning, especially, that time should be regarded as a time of rest, of relaxation or of unwinding. It is a time of not doing after all, a time of not being actively engaged in anything. From the start, then, find out how to let your practice proceed naturally, rather than seeking to make things happen through an act of determination. You might set aside ten minutes within which to practice and then extend the time a minute or two with each subsequent sitting, until you are sitting for thirty or forty minutes at a time; and you should find a place where you can be assured that you can continue to do so at the same time and place each day, because we are, very much, creatures of habit. In fact, when you wake up, and while you are still in bed, you should place your palms over your solar plexus and then guide them slowly down to your lower abdomen. Do this several times, and then go to the bathroom to relieve yourself, brush your teeth and bathe, and then sit down to practice. This routine can be used at other times during the day as well, and, when established, it becomes as natural as brushing your teeth. What is most important, however, is that you make it a living experience, a time of discovery through relaxation and passive observation.

Eating is one of our earliest sources of conditioning, and so part of your practice is to regard food as medicine. This may seem to be a simple enough thing to do, but it can prove to be very trying. For many, this simple practice is thoroughly disruptive, producing feelings of deprivation and anxiety when they no longer have access to their private pacifiers or conditioning. One of its purposes, however, is to reveal those attachments, in order to discover the natural inclination to be a part of them, and then have that awareness evolve into freedom.

As to the procedure itself, do not eat directly before you sit, because it may make you sleepy. If you have eaten too much, you may be thoroughly distracted by the discomfort of feeling full, perhaps even to the point of finding it hard to breathe. However, not eating enough has its disadvantages, too, making you feel weak, have headaches and be incapable of concentration. You must learn to listen to your needs. You must be aware of what happens to you all the time, so that you can know the right food, the right amount of it to eat and, also, discover how long to wait after having eaten before sitting.

In this way, you may find that life takes on a sense of order, that you are not so involved in eating anymore, and, as a bonus perhaps, that you are losing weight. With only the most superficial observation, you may discover that eating as you do ordinarily may be followed by a plethora of such symptoms as vague feelings of unrest, headaches, depression, anxiety, stomachaches, muddled thinking, fatigue or itching. If you can detect what the causes are, you may be able to rid yourself of the symptoms. However, that may not prove to be as easy as it may seem. There are many kinds of addiction, but it is characteristic of them all, according to a current theory regarding what is involved in allergy, that you crave the very things that cause your problems. Sitting passively aware of everything that is transpiring, you relax. This not only serves to reduce your reactions overall, but also helps you to become less attached to things that have been troubling you. You become aware of how everything has happened, and, by not acting on it, come to tune in to an inner knowing that chimes in to help liberate you, as it were. It cannot be said too often that *you must find out what is best for you.* Some people require an empty stomach. Others prefer to shower and meditate an hour after eating lightly, and, to complicate matters, it may not always work for them. It's all there before one to observe. *All it takes is being aware of what's happening all the time.*

Anyone who has missed a night or two of sleep and has had to work knows how miserable it can be just to stay awake, let alone concentrate and, perhaps, do physical labor as well. Sleeping too much can make you feel sluggish, and so neither too much nor too little sleep is good for meditation. So there it is again! It is up to you, the practitioner, to find out what is best. Then, once you have done that, you can work out a schedule.

For example, you might sit from nine to ten in the evening, retiring directly afterwards. Arising at six in the morning, you can go about your morning ablutions and sit again before going out for the day. Should you awaken at night and find that you are not sleepy or that you have trouble falling asleep again, you can use that time as an opportunity to meditate. Sleep usually ensues as relaxation sets in. Should it not, however, then simply continue to sit. With practice, your need for sleep diminishes, and you may find that you can manage quite well on just four or five hours, or even less. In fact, there are meditators on record who no longer have any need to sleep but meditate instead. This ability is not something that can be forced or even learned but develops naturally.

Perseverance

Beginners often find that sitting practice is very uncomfortable. In fact, some may even continue to feel that way long past the time that they qualify as beginners. What keeps them coming back is perseverance. To make progress you must persevere, and you must sit every day at the same time and in the same place, relaxed and gently erect, simply aware of whatever is happening or lightly engaged in concentration and free of any sense of coercion.

Results

Looking for results is counterproductive. Ideally, all thought falls away and is replaced by a natural state, which, incidentally, proves to be healthy because it is free of desire and, thus, relatively free of stress. Having no aim is refreshing but is seldom understood, as such, and difficult for most to come by. The desires to do, to excel and to succeed are at the heart of one's very being. To relinquish such inclinations would seem to be outside the scope of what one can do, because it would take away the illusion of control. That is why a correct understanding of the Dharma is so important.

No Concern

Drop all cares! Put away all things during your practice and simply regulate your breath and mind. Then, even deluded thoughts are seen to come and go. Not caring about them, your mind grows calm. Close your eyes while sitting, and you won't see outside things. Sounds may still be evident, and you may feel that they are disturbing and that your practice is difficult; but in that very moment, if you are aware of what you are thinking as just thinking or of what you are hearing as just hearing, your problems, as such, drop away.

Habits

It is not really enough just to do sitting practice; and it is certainly not enough if you are doing so only twice a day. You must be attentive to your conduct and constantly be on guard against falling into the trap of habitual behavior. This means that you must recognize and then seek to control your greed, anger and delusion, that you should do good, take refuge in the Three Treasures (Buddha, Dharma and Sangha), observe the five precepts (not to kill, steal, commit adultery, lie or ingest intoxicating substances), and that you should read, study and inquire to make clear what you understand of the Dharma to be able to set up and maintain Right Understanding and Right View. In this way, you can be more free of desire, be more able to concentrate, and, in time, have successful meditation take place.

Experiences Likely to Arise

Do not be upset if, while practicing, you suddenly grow very hot, perspire profusely, shake, perhaps even violently, hear what seems like all-pervading sound, find yourself assuming various positions without intending to and, possibly, see apparitions. Do not attempt to suppress any of these manifestations! However, most practitioners never have any such experiences, but, on the contrary, practice successfully and have the benefit of improved health as well. One might wax mysterious and say that it is due to karma, although that is really no more than saying that it is what it is. It should suffice to say that meditation can sometimes be attended by mental, emotional and physical effects that are transient, as long as there is no attempt to stop them. Should they upset you, just understand that everything is void and that even what seems to exist changes constantly. Keep in mind that nothing is real because nothing has any inherent nature; and so there is nothing to crave or to reject. It is with such a view that you may be free of grasping, and it is then that concentration should easily ensue. Without such a view, however, you are in danger of being trapped by whatever may seem important to you.

Dharma Master TaoYuan, in describing his style of practice, said that one who has *prajna* (wisdom) should arouse great compassion and make a great vow to attain samadhi, to convert sentient beings widely, and not to seek salvation for himself. He must also abandon all conditions, or, in other words, simply stop doing anything at all, neither differentiating body and mind nor motion and stillness. He should eat and sleep just enough to sustain health, and he should set aside a time and place to meditate each day, sitting in either the full or half-lotus position. Should he choose to sit in the full-lotus, he should place his left foot on top of his right thigh and his right foot on top of his left thigh. Respectively, he should then place the back of his right hand in the palm of his left and then put the back of his left hand on his left foot in the half-lotus, or on his two upturned feet in the full-lotus, touching his thumbs together ever so lightly.

Having established a stable and comfortable base, he should then lean forward and backward and sway from right to left, slowly, diminishing the swings until he finds a place of balance, where he feels that he is sitting easily and without strain. To assure himself that this is so, he can check to see if his ears are directly over his shoulders and whether his nose is in line with his navel. He should, however, not force himself to assume and maintain a position that is not natural for him. Should he want, eventually, to be able to sit erectly, he should devote time to doing just that, as a separate daily practice.

When he is then able to sit in that way without any thought having to be given to it, he can incorporate it into his concentration-practice time. He should then touch the tip of his tongue to his palate, just behind his upper front teeth and maintain this contact throughout the entire time that he is sitting. To keep from falling asleep, he has his eyes slightly open, directing his gaze downward through the space permitted by his lowered eyelids. Having so arranged himself, he sits, thinking of neither good nor evil. Should any such thoughts arise, however, he should be aware of them as simply thoughts.

Practicing in this fashion over a period of time, he naturally comes to be of *one mind* (a mind no longer occupied with objects). When this stage has been arrived at, the four elements — earth, water, fire, and air — are said to be automatically at ease, and he has reached the level of bliss. Becoming skilled in these ways, he attains to what is described as *great satisfaction*. If he is not so skilled, however, he is advised to concentrate on the one mind until he is successful in obtaining this *satisfaction*. When his practice period is over and he is ready to get up, he moves slowly. Thus, when he stands up, he does not disturb his deep concentration and can, in time, continue to maintain it at all times and in all places, *holding* it as though it were a small baby. As he continues in this way, the complete strength of dhyana should eventually become available to him.

It is easy to look for a pearl in calm water, but it is very hard to do so when there are large waves. The pearl of Mind appears, then, in the *clear water* of dhyana. In **The Complete Enlightenment Sutra**, it is written that *Ch'an Ting* (dhyana) gives rise to clear wisdom that is free of all obstruction, that is beyond everything, and that comes about more readily in the calm of meditation.

A question in **The Great Sastra** asks why the Buddha advises that one use only the lotus (or half-lotus) position. His reply was that, of all the methods that have been tried in meditation, the lotus position was found to be the most secure and stable, enabling the practitioner to sit for a long time without tiring; and so it is ideal for practicing Ch'an. It has a way of putting one's mind in order, too, just as it arranges one physically. Of the four mind avenues of practice-sitting, walking, standing and lying down. the lotus position is supreme, contributing to the most proper demeanor for practice.

There are heterodox practitioners who raise their feet, stand up often or bare their feet. Such conceited fellows exhibit unrest and cannot quiet their minds. This, then, is another reason why one should sit in the lotus position. Furthermore, sitting in this manner, it is easier for one to develop correct thought and correct concentration which can then lead to *oneness of mind*. Elsewhere in **The Great Sastra**, it is also advised that one who would learn to meditate should concentrate on one point, which should be either between the eyebrows or in the middle of the forehead.

The great T'ienT'ai master, ChihI, who taught Chih-Kuan and methods of practice in Ch'an, described in great detail how one should regulate one's diet to be fit to enter the Tao. Simply put, he said that if you eat too much at one time, your stomach will be so full that you will be unable to breathe properly. This, in turn, will cause your psychic centers to be blocked and your mind to be obstructed, making it extremely difficult, if not impossible, for you to practice. If, on the other hand, you have not eaten enough, this can cause your mind to be unsteady for want of energy. Naturally, these extreme conditions are to be avoided, and they suggest just two reasons why one should practice the Middle Way.

Regarding your diet, avoid food that only you can know is unsuitable for your practice, can keep the elements in disharmony and can lead to illness. This is a way of pointing out the practicality of being ever mindful, for it is through such observation that you can ultimately learn what is appropriate for you. It is not unheard of that certain foods cannot only make one feel out of sorts or ill, but also may cause one to have sudden mood swings or even hallucinations. Hence, the sutra says that if you are physically at ease, the Tao can prosper, and that if food and drink are properly regulated, happiness can be enjoyed in quiet and the still mind can make a great show of zeal.

Regulating Sleep

It is said that overindulgence in sleep results from ignorance, clouds the mind, and should be discouraged. He who sleeps too much will soon not only cast aside his practice of Dharma but will also quickly lose his ability to practice, as his mind becomes confused and all his good roots come to no avail. Therefore, one should awaken to the impermanence of life and regulate one's sleep in order to keep one's spirit high and one's mind clear for the purpose of abiding in the state that leads to the manifestation of imperturbable stillness. Hence, it is further said that self-cultivation should always go on and that excessive sleep should not be allowed to cause one's time to pass aimlessly. One should think of the destructive fire of impermanence that scorches the whole world and strive to be liberated from it as soon as possible, instead of indulging oneself in excessive sleep.

Regulating Body, Breath and Mind

Body, breath and mind are all interdependent and are sometimes conceived of as being aspects of the same thing. In Buddhism, there are practices that have been devised to work with these aspects. Also, there are methods that are designed to take you through preliminary, intermediate, and final practices. These methods and practices are employed to prepare you to enter into and to come out of, some say, the heart of it all meditation. Your everyday activity must have a gentle quality. If there is any roughness to it, your breath is made rough as well; and when your breath is rough, your mind is unsettled, so that when you attempt to sit, you become perplexed and uneasy. To remedy this, simply visualize yourself as being already physically relaxed and sitting at ease before you actually sit down to practice. When the beneficial effects of this simple procedure have manifested and you feel warm and relaxed and gently present, you can arrange yourself in your chosen sitting position.

What follows are directions for sitting in the half-lotus position, as described by yet another teacher. Arrange your cushions so that you can sit comfortably for a long time. Then, position yourself in the half-lotus position. To do this, sit upright with your knees out to either side and your legs crossed at your ankles. Then place your left lower limb on top of your right thigh and slide your left lower leg in close to your lower belly, so that the sole of your left foot is turned up and the toes of your left foot are parallel to your right thigh. The toes of your right foot are also arranged so that they are parallel to your left thigh.

Should you want to sit in the full-lotus position, observe the above procedure; and then place your right lower leg on your left, turning the sole of your right foot up and drawing it in close to your lower belly. Once settled, loosen your belt just enough to keep it from slipping and then loosen anything else that might be even slightly binding, like a wristwatch or a snug collar. When you have done that, lay the back of your left hand in the upturned palm of your right, and rest the back of your right hand on the upturned soles of your feet. Then check to see if you are leaning, slumping or straining, and, having made whatever adjustments you need, shake your limbs seven or eight times to relax them. Then check again to see how you are sitting, making sure that you are not slumped down or sitting rigidly upright but are easily erect. Your head should not jut forward or lean to one side or the other, and your chin should not be vigorously pulled in. You should feel that you are just sitting naturally. Then, slowly and continuously exhale through your mouth, while imagining that all the waste and impurities that might be in your psychic centers are being expelled along with your breath. Close your mouth, so that your upper lip and teeth meet your lower ones and your tongue touches your palate, and then close your eyes and inhale *clean air* through your nostrils. Now, imagine that you are a mountain, settled and immobile. Sitting in this way, you can avoid both strain and slackness.

Regulating the Breath

For meditation successfully to take place, the breath must first be regulated. There are, traditionally, four kinds of breath: *audible, gasping, coarse* and *restful*. The first three are considered to be somewhat disruptive. If you can hear your breath, it is said to be *audible*. If it is not audible, and is also obstructed or not free, it is called *gasping breath*. If the breath is neither *audible* nor fine, it is said to be *coarse*. When it is neither *audible* nor *gasping* nor *coarse*, but continuous, being barely perceptible and so fine that it is almost imperceptible and also accompanied by comfort and ease, it is called *restful breath*. An *audible breath* scatters your composure; a *gasping breath* ties you up; a *coarse breath* tires you; but a *restful breath* indicates a quiet mind. If any of the first three ways of breathing is present, it means that your breath is not yet regulated.

Regulating the Breath: a Summary

There are three notable phases that take place during the course of this practice:

Concentrating properly, you relax.

Your mind grows calm as you relax more and more.

You have the experience of breathing through all your pores.

Entering Meditation

The purpose or goal, is to reduce confusion and thinking, to keep your attention from wandering and to stabilize the mind when it starts sinking, floating, straining or becoming too diffuse.

Sinking mind is dull, confused and untraceable. Even dozing may occur. Therefore, to remedy this, you are advised to fix your attention on the tip of your nose.

Floating mind drifts; you feel uneasy and are concerned about externals. Therefore, you are advised to fix your attention on your navel because this has been found to keep thoughts from arising. This accomplished, the mind is said to be stabilized and is calmed easily. It then becomes a *regulated mind*.

Sustained Meditation

Meditation ultimately is simply awareness without intention. However, you are encouraged to be constantly aware and to know whether your body, breath and mind are properly regulated. If, after having regulated your body and having sat for a while, you notice that your sitting has become strained or loose, that you are inclined to one side, drooping, holding your shoulders up or pulling them backward or forward, or that you are somehow not just right, you should make the proper adjustments in order to maintain a *regulated mind*. It might be possible, however, that even though your body is regulated, your breath is not, even after you have already dealt with various unregulated aspects of the breath, which may be audible, gasping or coarse. It may also happen that, even though the body and breath are regulated, the mind is either floating, sinking, loose, strained or unsettled, in which case the methods mentioned earlier should then be used to regulate the mind. Although these methods are to be used expediently, rather than in succession, they may, nevertheless, seem very willful. Actually, it is a little like learning to ride a bicycle; once learned, it takes care of itself.

Coming Out of Meditation

Before your meditation session is over, you should, in a manner of speaking, put it aside and exhale, using your mouth while visualizing the air leaving your psychic centers. Then gently rotate your shoulders, arms, hands, head and neck; next wiggle your toes to relax them. Having done this, rub your body with your hands, and then rub your palms together and put them over your eyes, cupping them for a while. Finally when you feel that you have cooled down sufficiently, you can leave your seat. To come out of meditation abruptly, even though everything may have been stabilized while you were sitting, can cause headaches and all sorts of illness.

The Practice of Chih-Kuan in Relation to Coarse and Distracted Mind

When a beginner sits down to practice, his or her mind is usually coarse and unsettled. Practicing *Chih* is conducive to mind control, but, failing that, one can switch to *Kuan*. Let us see what it all means.

The first approach, called *Chih*, has three components, as follows:

According to the sutra, a fixed mind that cannot stray is like a bound monkey. As applied to practice, it means fixing your attention on the tip of your nose, on your navel, or an inch and a half below it.

The sutra further says that the five sense organs are controlled by the mind. To stop a wandering mind, you restrain it through observation as it moves.

Understanding is of primary importance. Referring to the sutra again, we find that the causes that create phenomena are ownerless and empty. Whoever calms his/her mind, has the foundation for monastic practice. Stopping all arising causes and ensures the attainment of Absolute Reality by means of the realization that all things (dharmas) arise from the mind, that their existence is due to circumstantial causes and that they are devoid of separate self. If this is understood, the mind will not grasp at anything, and its stirredup condition will simply come to a complete stop. The term Chih means just that – *stopping*.

The second approach, called Kuan, has two components, as follows:

If you find yourself caught in sexual desire, for example, you should cultivate the opposite view, seeing sex as dirty and ugly.

When you are consumed with anger, you have to find a way to express compassion instead. The opposite of an attachment to the ego's concerns would be to call to mind how everything is an illusion. When you are deluged with thoughts, you count your breaths. The effect of this strategy is, ultimately, to call a halt to discrimination.

This consists of looking into the nature of things and seeing that they have no inherent existence and that their apparent existence is dependent upon apparent causes, which, in turn, are dependent upon past experiences and what is presumed to be present circumstances. In other words, causes, also, have no inherent nature; and so they are actually identical with the undifferentiated reality from which they seemingly arise. Since the objects, thus contemplated, are unreal, it then follows that the mind which contemplated them will cease to arise.

The Chih-Kuan Dharma Gate

To recapitulate, remember that in order to prepare for meditation you should sit properly and regulate your breath to stabilize and control your mind. This requires a great deal of patience for most practitioners because the mind is, ordinarily, quite unruly. Not succeeding at it should not keep you from doing *Chih-Kuan*, however; nor does it mean that you should quit your practice of regulating your body, speech and mind. As it is, you soon discover that the mind's activity is like a monkey, never stopping for an instant. The advice that is traditionally given is to limit this monkey's movement. The *Chih*, in *Chih-Kuan* means *stopping* and refers to stopping the false or misleading activity of the mind. To do this — i.e., to tether the *monkey mind* by practicing *Chih* - the first step is to fix the mind on a single object to keep it from wandering from one object to another. Having accomplished this, you *look within* to contemplate your thoughts. There, you discover anew that they arise in great number and often without any relatedness, appearing, for the most part, randomly. You also realize that future thoughts have not yet come. When you ask yourself which of these thoughts is your mind, you realize that your *false mind* rises and falls and is, thus, also devoid of reality. If you continue in this way, you become familiar with this unreality, and your false mind comes to an end by itself; and with the *false mind* at an end, reality is evident.

When you first sit down to practice, your mind is often unsettled. This is appropriately called *unsettled mind*, and to set it at rest, *stopping*, or *Chih*, is used. If it is stopped again and again, the thinking process gradually comes to an end. While meditating, you may find yourself getting drowsy. This is called *sinking mind* and the way to awaken it is by contemplation, or Kuan, which involves closing your eyes and looking inward, as it were, to the source of your thoughts. There are three kinds of Kuan, or contemplation: contemplation of the void; contemplation of the unreal; and contemplation of the mean.

Contemplation of the Void

You look into all things within the universe, from the largest including the earth, mountains and rivers — to the smallest — including your body and mind. Doing so, you perceive that everything changes in every instant and is non-existent and void; and when your mind looks into this voidness, that is called *contemplation of the void*.

Contemplation of the Unreal

When you are familiar with this *contemplation of the void*, you look into your mind or the place, as it were, from which thoughts arise, and you find that each thought has its object. You then realize that every phenomenon- owes its existence to a union of an inner cause and an outer concurring circumstance. For instance, a grain of rice sprouts because of the union of an inner direct cause, which is the seed, with an outer concurring condition, in the form of the water and mud that moisten and nourish it. If the grain of rice is not sown and is left in the warehouse, it will never sprout because there is only an inner, direct cause without an outer condition. Also, if there are only water and mud, without the seed being sown, they, alone, cannot produce the sprout because there has been no union with an original cause namely, the seed. Every phenomenon- in the world is created by the union of direct and circumstantial causes and vanishes as soon as they are separated. This includes thoughts that arise and disappear in the mind and that cannot be grasped. Such contemplation is called looking into the unreal.

Contemplation of the Mean

There are two contrasting attitudes connected with *contemplation of the void*, on the one hand, and *looking into the unreal*, on the other. When you reach this stage, your achievement is still incomplete. Having succeeded with *contemplation of the void*, do not cling to the void; and when you have achieved contemplation of the unreal, do not grasp at the unreal. When you succeed in keeping from the extremes of the void and the unreal, your non-relying and non-clinging mind will be extraordinarily clear, and this stage is called, *contemplation of the mean*.

At first glance, the *Chih-Kuan* Dharma Gate seems to imply diverse or successive stages. In practice, the use of either *Chih* or *Kuan* depends solely on the inclinations of the mind during meditation. As a matter of fact, the purpose of *Chih* is to return all thoughts to one, *the one mind*, and that of *Kuan* is to attain clear insight into the truth, which is to be free of illusion. When *stopping*, or *Chih*, is practiced, it should not stray from *stopping*. Do not cling to the printed word, but practice intelligently, according to the circumstances.

The breath is the source of life. When the breath stops, the body is just an inanimate corpse. With the nervous system no longer functioning, the mind vanishes and life comes to an end. That is why life is said to be preserved by the breath, which links the body with the mind. Thus, we see that a human being is composed of body, breath and mind and that the breath plays the important role of uniting the other two components.

The T'ien T'ai meditation manual, entitled **The Six Profound Dharma Gates (T'ung Meng Chih-Kuan)**, focuses on breathing as a comprehensive practice that may be preceded by training in the *Chih-Kuan* method, or it can be used independently of it. The consecutive stages are as follows:

Counting the breath

Following the breath

Stopping (*Chih*)

Contemplation (*Kuan*)

Returning

Purification

The Method of Counting the Breath

The breath counting method offers two possibilities, as follows: After you have regulated your breath, so that it is neither too tight nor too loose, count slowly from one to ten on *either* your inhalation or exhalation. Do not count on both. For example, breathing in, count one; then exhale and upon inhaling again, count two, and so on. Your mind soon becomes fixed on the activity and does not wander as readily. If it wanders off before you have reached the count of ten, return gently and without further thought to one, and resume counting as described above. This is the method of meditation known as *Breath Counting*.

Realization Attained Through Breath Counting

As you grow accustomed to the method just described, your breath becomes finer and finer, until it seems to be non-existent. This stage is called *Realization by Breath Counting*.

The Method of Following the Breath

This method is both easy and simple: Just focus on your breath and follow it mindfully, holding on gently, until it is no longer an issue. Then mind and breath become one.

Realization Attained Through Following the Breath

As it follows the breath, your mind becomes increasingly subtle. You may notice, at first, the length of your breath; but as it gets more refined it becomes almost undetectable, and at that point it feels as though it is occurring through the pores of your skin. The effect on your mind is stilling or calming. At this stage of practice, you may wish to cultivate your breath further. Your next step will be the practice of *stopping*, also consisting of two phases: *Chih* and *Kuan*.

The Practice of Stopping, or Chih

Focus lightly on the tip of your nose; it leads to *stopping*. In the course of this simple practice, you may suddenly feel as if your body and mind have vanished; you will, thereby, enter a state of stillness called *dhyana*.

Realization Attained Through the Practice of Chih

At this stage, clarity develops through awareness. You feel no longer attached to anything, and there is no longer a sense of subject and object while sitting; then you proceed to the stage called *Kuan*.

The Practice of Contemplation, or Kuan

This practice consists of a gentle, passive observation of your refined breathing, regarding it as a movement in a void that has no reality of its own.

Realization Attained Through the Practice of Kuan

This is a further refinement of practice in which you come to feel as though you are breathing through the pores of your skin. To a bystander, you may appear as if you are not breathing. When you reach this stage, *Chih* and *Kuan* become indistinguishable. As a point of interest, the *Samatha Vipasyana* for beginners differs from *Chih-Kuan* in intent, in that the former develops mindfulness, while the latter develops absorption. An extended session of contemplation should be followed by *Returning*.

The Method of Returning

Contemplating your breath, you may realize that there is an apparently subjective mind that contemplates an apparently objective breath and that these very clearly constitute the two poles, the essence, of duality. However, they are to be returned, as it were, to the one, fundamental Mind.

Realization Attained Through the Method of Returning

This method develops the awareness of the *knower* that contemplates the breath as rising and falling with the mind. This rising and falling mind is experienced to be like the waves that rise and fall in the sea, and this leads to a realization of the illusory nature of it all. The waves are not the water, the fundamental face of which can be seen only after the waves have subsided. Similarly, the mind that rises and falls, like the waves in the water, is not the True Mind. Now look into this True Mind, which is uncreated. Because it is uncreated, it is beyond is and is *not*; and it is, therefore, void. Because it is void, it follows that there is no subjective mind that contemplates. Because there is no contemplating mind, it follows that there is no object contemplated; and because knowledge and its object vanish, this is called *The Realization of Returning Method*. Following that realization, the idea of returning remains; to relinquish it, one should meditate on purity.

Realization of the State of Purity

The practice of purification consists of contemplation on discriminating views. When the mind is still like calm water and there is an absence of false thinking, the Real Mind, which does not exist apart from false thinking, manifests. This water without waves sort of Mind is called *The Realization of Purity*.

These *Six Profound Dharma Gates* may be seen as consisting of a preliminary set of methods, involving *counting* and *following* the breath, the two main practices of *Chih* and *Kuan*, and the concluding practices of *returning* and *purifying*. More specifically, stopping (*Chih*) is the chief practice, while contemplation (*Kuan*) is its support, until perception is realized, which means that one is no longer involved in making distinctions or having attachments. This reference to perception refers to the *five skandhas*, wherein it is seen that distinctions are made at the level of conception. Thus, no longer being at that level is to be at the more subtle level of *perceptions* (again relating to the *five skandhas*).

To realize Great Dhyana and Great Prajna, the mind must be at ease. *The Six Profound Dharma Gates* process contains methods that are designed to regulate the mind, enabling it to relax. This is paramount, for if you do not know how to relax, you cannot even begin to practice. Having learned to relax, then, and with mind and breath regulated, meditation can take place. It is then that you can practice *The Six Profound Dharma Gates* of counting, following, stopping, contemplating, returning and purifying, going through all of them over and over again, slowly and patiently, putting your mind ever more at ease as you let go more and more. To follow any strict order of practice at this time is counterproductive. If you find that counting the breath goes well for you, count your breath. If the purifying method seems called for and works well for you, do that. Then, in only a few days, you may be able to understand your mind easily as never before.

Meditation and Ch'an Ting

Suffice it to say that there are many approaches to meditation in Buddha-dharma that are to be found under the headings of *Ch'an* and *Ch'an Ting*. *Ch'an Ting* alone is an umbrella name for many methods: the Four Dhyanas, the Four Infinities, the FourVoid Worldly Ch'an, the Nine Observations, the Samadhi of Nine Degrees (supramundane), the Ch'an of self-nature and the Ch'an Ting. These approaches can lead one to deep dhyana, where real wisdom is to be found; and with real wisdom, there can be self enlightenment, enlightenment of others and the Ultimate Perfect Enlightenment.

It has been suggested that to sit alone in a forest or on some remote mountainside to meditate would seem to abnegate the Bodhisattva vow of saving all sentient beings. In answer to that, consider that even a Bodhisattva who is far away from all sentient beings still retains them in his mind. Therefore, it is in this way, when you meditate in the quiet *place* of *Ch'an Ting* and have acquired real Wisdom, that you can *truly* help sentient beings. If you are still curious as to why you must practice in solitude, consider this analogy. It is somewhat like trying to light a lamp in a strong wind, as opposed to taking it to a room where the air is still. Just as it is so very difficult, if not impossible, to light a lamp in a storm, it is equally hard to find wisdom in a disordered mind. Thus, even Bodhisattvas live apart from sentient beings and stay in quiet places, so that they can practice *Ch'an Ting* and develop and purify their wisdom.

You have to concentrate or focus your attention on whatever you do in the everyday world, if you want to do it properly. The same applies to the quiet inner world, as well, although not in quite the same way. To make another analogy, let us say that you have a lamp that is in good working order and that all the surrounding conditions contribute to its producing a good, bright light. It is only then that you will have a good, bright light. However, the practice of Buddha-dharma assuredly is far more subtle than the act of lighting a lamp. The mind of confusion is much lighter than even the lightest feather and moves so swiftly that it is gone before anything can be done about it. It cannot be controlled, because any such attempt is, in itself, an act of confusion. As quickly as lightning, the objects of the mind appear and disappear, and this frenetic activity does not stop. Indeed, it cannot stop! The only way out of this tangle is made possible through meditation.

In **The Commentary on the Dhyana Paramita**, it is written that a Bodhisattva must abandon his family and all his worldly possessions, be ready to give up his very life, and then stay in a quiet place to prepare his mind for dhyana by remaining still and calm in body and mind. When he is free of thought, there is no way for evil to arise. In preparing for dhyana, one must endure whatever happens, never tiring, always persevering. When confronted with evil (an obstacle to samadhi), he must exercise great patience in not responding with the defilement of anger. This is accomplished by not discriminating and by neither grasping at nor rejecting anything. In his quest for dhyana, he concentrates on the one Mind (the one mind being no-mind). Nothing sways him from his course. He sits, never lying down, sits even though tired, never resting; and, though seemingly gaining nothing by his apparent efforts, he, thereby shows, indeed, his great progress. A Bodhisattva practices and completes all of the Six Paramitas, concentrates on the one Mind, which is no-mind, and can finally understand all the aspects of birth and death in the world through Prajna.

Counting the Breath

All of the Six Wonderful and Profound Dharma Gates can produce many kinds of dhyana. The first of these is attained by the practice of counting the breath, because, in this way, you will arrive at the Four Dhyanas of Form, the Four Immeasurable Minds and the Four Formless Dhyanas. When you have attained the last stage of *Neither Thinking Nor Not Thinking is Not Nirvana*, you have only attained *The Way of The Three Vehicles*, because this worldly *Ch'an Ting* is not yet real, still having some defilement. Using The Wonderful Dharma Gate of counting the breath and neither discriminating nor grasping, you can attain all three Vehicles at the level of Hinayana.

Following The Breath

By this second practice, you can produce the Sixteen Special Dharmas:

When inhaling, knowing that you are inhaling;
When exhaling, knowing that you are exhaling;
Knowing when you are breathing a long or a short breath;
Knowing the whole body as the breath;

Knowing the movement of the body;

Knowing the delight of the mind;

Knowing the happiness of the mind;

Knowing mind activity;

Knowing comfort of the mind;

Knowing concentration of the mind;

Knowing freedom of mind;

Knowing impermanence;

Knowing all things (dharmas) as dispersed;

Knowing desirelessness;

Knowing nothingness or the property of vanishing;

Knowing what it is to abandon and give up everything.

Stopping

If you practice *stopping*, you can obtain five kinds of dhyana, as follows:

EarthWheel Samadhi (which is not yet to have arrived at the *tenth stage*);

Water Wheel Samadhi (which enables you to have good conditions for all kinds of Dhyanas);

Space Wheel Samadhi (which consists of five expedient ways of dhyana practice, whereby you come to understand space as being without any nature);

The Wheel of Golden Sand Samadhi (which frees you from misleading views, so that you no longer grasp after right wisdom);

The Wheel of Diamond Samadhi (which is also known as *The CompletelyWithoutObstacles Tao*, a practice that lets you sever your bondage to the three realms of desire, form and formlessness forever).

Furthermore, by *stopping*, you can attain Birthless Wisdom, whereby you can gain entrance to Nirvana.

Contemplation

Through contemplation, you can take part in the Nine Thinkings, the Eight Lines of Thought, the Freedom From Eight Forms, the Eight Stages of Mental Concentration, the Ten Universals, the Samadhi of the Nine Degrees, the Samadhi of the Powerful Lion's Roar, the Transcendental Samadhi, the Practice of Ch'an, the Fourteen Transmutations of Mind, the Triple Bright Samadhi, the Six Transcendental Powers, and the Eight Liberations, all of which enable you to acquire the Samadhi of No Sensation and No Thought.

Returning

The meditator, through Prajna, is freed of defilements by returning to the void of the Original Source, which is no source and in which there is nothing but void without form and with non-action indicating an absence of self-nature. Without any self-nature, there is no longer a subject or an object, and distinctions are no longer made because there is no one to make them and nothing to make them about.

In this way, the thirty-seven conditions leading to Bodhi are satisfied, as well as those contained in the Four Noble Truths, the Twelve Nidanas and in the Right Contemplation of the Middle Way, whereby Nirvana can be attained.

Purification

If a meditator knows, through Prajna, that all Dharmas are originally pure, he can acquire the Dhyana of self-nature because he has attained what is known as Hinayana Nirvana, or TwoVehicles Nirvana. If a Bodhisattva can enter the stage of the IronWheel King, has completed the Ten Grades of Bodhisattva Faith and continues to practice, he can produce the following nine kinds of Great Dhyana:

Self-Nature Dhyana

All Kinds of Dhyana

Difficult Dhyana

All-Kinds-of-Doors Dhyana

Good-Person Dhyana

All-Active Dhyana

Rid-of-Defilement Dhyana

The-Joy-of-this-Life-and-The-Next-Life Dhyana

Pure-and-Clean Dhyana (Since a Bodhisattva depends on this kind of Dhyana, he can attain The Fruit of Great Bodhi Nirvana)

In Sudden Enlightenment, the nature of mind is realized as being originally pure.

Dharmas are neither grasped at nor rejected; there is neither being nor non-being; there is neither birth nor death; there is neither this nor that; and there is neither void nor existence, Then, there is the knowing afforded by the awareness of non-duality, where nothing is grasped, there being neither someone to grasp nor anything to grasp at. If Original Substance is known, there is freedom from attachment to the objects of the sense organs. Once there is no longer any illusion of the existence of a permanent self, there are no longer any encumbrances. There is no grasping at the void and no holding to stillness; there is simply whatever is, without defining or choosing. Short of this, there might still be a somewhat encumbered level of awareness where there is a recognition of still being in the midst of causes and conditions, without attachment; but it is to be understood that even this recognition is a kind of grasping.

The Sastra of Entering The Tao of Sudden Enlightenment, by Ch'an Master Hui Hai of the T'ang Dynasty, asks what method should be used to understand Original Dharma. The reply is that one need only to practice dhyana. Referring to **The Sutra of the Ch'an Door**, one reads that if you seek the wisdom of the Buddha, you need *Ch'anTing*; for without it, you will have a great abundance of false thoughts and will be in danger of destroying your good roots. To understand this more clearly, *Ch'anTing* is defined as follows: When there are no false thoughts, that is *Ch'an*; and to see one's Original Nature is *Ting*.

Original Nature is also known as non-Birth, or Unborn Mind, where there is no longer any *one* to be moved by the eight winds of gain, loss, defamation, fame, praise, ridicule, sorrow and joy. Thus, even if one is worldly but attains *Ting*, he already approaches being a Buddha.

Elsewhere it is written that if you are free of attachment and if you no longer think of things (dharmas) during meditation nor discriminate between good and evil, then past things are past. If you do not think of them, the mind of the past vanishes. This is called *no past*. Furthermore, the future has not yet arrived; and when it is not necessary to wish to obtain it, the mind of the future is no more. This is called *no future*. Finally, the present is already present, and there is no need to grasp at anything. When you are free of thoughts, there is no longer any grasping. Without grasping, the mind of the present vanishes. This is called *no present*. Then your mind dwells on nothing, and this is Original Mind and Original Nature. This Mind that dwells on nothing is the Mind of the Buddha, the Mind of liberation and the Mind of nobirth. Ch'an Master KueiFeng said that *True Nature* is neither pure nor impure and that there is no difference between the holy and the worldly.

Varieties of Ch'an

Master KueiFeng, also, said that when shallow and deep stages of Ch'an are referred to and that when a person chooses to practice the deep ones because he looks down on the *shallow* stages and then finds a way to do so, what he engages in is called heterodox Ch'an. Holding to cause and effect and practicing with like and dislike are known as Worldly People Ch'an. However, when only the illusion of the personal self has been eliminated through Enlightenment but not that of the self-nature of dharmas (things), this is called Hinayana Ch'an. On the other hand, when the ego and all dharmas are enlightened, this is called Mahayana Ch'an. Here, the self-nature of one's self and the self-nature of everything else, or all dharmas, are known to be unreal. If one's own mind is suddenly enlightened, it is in its original purity, free of defilement and not outside the stream. This mind is the Buddha, and practicing in this manner is called Supreme Ch'an.

The Sixth Patriarch, HuiNeng, described *sitting Ch'an* by stating that being without obstacles in the Dharma and being beyond all ideas of good and evil, without a single thought arising, is called *sitting*, whereas seeing into the stillness of one's Original Nature is called *Ch'an*. Regarding *Ch'anTing*, he said that the absence of external form (i.e., no object) is *Ch'an*, and to be free of the confusion of thought (i.e., no subject) is *Ting*. Furthermore, he said that if one grasps the forms (the apparent objects outside), this is evidence of a confused mind and adds to the confusion of what the mind conceives of as being inside. If one is no longer attached to objects and to there being an outside, then there is no longer any such confusion of mind. Original Nature is pure and still, but is disturbed by thinking and, it follows, by objects. When there are no things, no outside and no confusion in the mind, that is real *Ting*. **The Sutra of Bodhisattva Discipline** is a bit more succinct. There, it simply says that originally your own nature is clean and pure.

Observing the Mind

We are ordinarily concerned with things that are conceived of as being outside of us, or, essentially, the objects of our thoughts; and we never think of observing the place within, as it were, whence thoughts seem to arise. By looking inward at the source of thought, the workings of your mind are still evident but are no longer so commanding, and a more and more passive sort of observation develops that reduces false thought and can help to reveal your own True Nature. In all Mahayana sutras, it can be seen that Prajna (Wisdom) must be accompanied by Universal Illumination. In one such sutra entitled ***Observing the Ground of the Mind***, it is stated that one who observes the mind can be liberated but that one who does not is always bound by birth and death. Along somewhat similar lines, one finds in **The Sutra of Nirvana** that Supreme Dhyana is described as observing the nature of the mind. *Chih-Kuan*, in Buddha-dharma, is translated as either *Dhyana* and *Wisdom* (*Ting-Hui*) or *Stillness* and *Illumination*. In The **MahaChih-Kuan** the stillness of Dharma Nature is called *Chih*, and stillness with illumination is called *Kuan*; and it concludes, therefore, that *Chih-Kuan* is the supreme method for purifying the mind. There are, however, many ways to practice *Chih-Kuan*. Just to mention a few, there are *Deep and Shallow, Sudden and Gradual, Cultivation and Principles* and *Complete and Incomplete*; and to complicate matters even further, there are three different categories of *Chih-Kuan* in the T'ien T'ai tradition: gradual, unfixed and perfect.

Gradual Chih-Kuan

In **The Commentary on the Dhyana Paramita of Gradual Chih-Kuan**, practice is described as being shallow at first and deep later, which implies a gradual development. Understanding, however, is said to come suddenly.

Unfixed Chih-Kuan

Unfixed Chih-Kuan, also known as *The Six Wonderful Dharma Gates*, is sometimes described as the *step by step* method leading to sudden understanding. Here, practice is gradual at first and then sudden.

Perfect Chih-Kuan

In **The Maha-Chih-Kuan**, it says that in Perfect and Sudden Chih-Kuan, all conditions and reality are merely three contemplations in one mind, and that there is only sudden understanding and action, with no distinction as to when it began or as to how it progressed thereafter.

The practices of The Maha-Chih-Kuan method are thorough, assuredly, but are too subtle to be done without the aid of an accomplished teacher. However, until such time as the reader may discover such a teacher, he might practice the following effective method of observing the mind. Sit comfortably in the lotus position or in any other position that is suitable for you. Lay down all things, and even give up the thought of laying everything down. In this way, thinking of neither good nor evil, close your eyes gently and lightly observe where your thoughts seem to issue from. This permits you passively to be aware of your false thoughts as they suddenly come and just as suddenly go, neither grasping at them nor driving them away; thus, in time, you can come to understand profoundly that false thought has no self-nature (is empty) and that it is originally void. When false thought is then illuminated by your mind, a stillness becomes evident, which then becomes *suchness*. Then if another thought suddenly arises, using the same approach, just observe lightly to see where the thought seems to come from. Do this at least once a day for at least half an hour.

If you continue to reinforce your knowledge of Buddha-dharma, as well, through reading and finding people who are inclined to hear what you might have to say about Buddhism or practice, then, over a period of time, this meditation can help reduce false thought (known as *using wisdom to support Ting*) and increase the power of illumination (known as *using Ting to beget wisdom*). If you continue in this way, you will, eventually, be able to sit without a single thought arising. When there is awareness, with no dwelling and no grasping, the source of mind is void and still. Then, Wisdom (Prajna) and Original Nature respond as one from moment to moment.

In **The Hand-Flower Sutra**, it states that when you observe the mind, you see the birth and death of thought after thought as having the quality of being magical and unreal. The subject of Wisdom is Prajna, which is like saying that Prajna is Wisdom, while its object is ignorance (confusion or false thought). The perfume of Prajna is then said to permeate ignorance more and more until there is just Prajna and a return to Original Nature. Whether walking, sitting or lying down, one should always be aware of the Substance (stillness) of Original Nature.

The function of illumination is Enlightenment, which is sometimes referred to as *right thought about reality*.

It is like a pearl that emits light and, thereby, also illuminates the substance of the pearl. If a false thought arises in an illuminated mind, it vanishes as quickly as a snowflake in a blazing furnace. Then, even strong habits no longer present any obstacles. With such practice, your Original Nature appears stronger and stronger. There should be no *need* or *intention* to have illumination, because need and intention stand in the way of its ever coming about.

When there is real illumination, there is no longer any involvement with words. Then, mind is no-mind. Then, there is simply *Suchness*. Without thought, there are no conditions; and Original Nature, known directly, *is* reality. However, even if you can concentrate on one thought and observe the mind for just a moment or two, you still have benefited by knowing Prajna, and have, thereby, planted the seed of Bodhi.

In **The Lankavatara Sutra**, it says that you should rely fully on the teachings and then find a quiet place where, practicing free of all doubt, there can be Enlightenment.

In **The Sutra of Complete Enlightenment**, it says that all Tathagatas arise from the ground cause of correct practice; and so, again and again, proper understanding and right practice are advised.

Conclusion

We have seen that there are many ways to bring about meditation in the Buddhist tradition and that they can bestow upon a practitioner all around emotional, mental and physical health, enabling him to gain Enlightenment and, thereby, benefiting both himself and others. There is the proviso, however, that even though sitting practice can promote good health, health is beneficial only temporarily; because, no matter how long you live, you must finally die.

In **The Sutra of Complete Enlightenment**, it says that since time without beginning, all sentient beings have been mired in ignorance. In their confusion they have mistaken the four elements (earth, water, fire, air) for their bodies and the shadows of the data of their six conditioned senses for their minds. The aim, then, is to be free of those delusions, going from confusion to Enlightenment. To keep that aim alive, it is important to use sutras and anything else that helps to clarify Buddha-dharma and to continue to practice discipline and concentration in order to develop expert meditation so that Prajna can arise.

Recommended Postures

Full Lotus

Full Lotus (side view)

Half Lotus

Half Lotus (side view)

Meditation Styles and Techniques

The first thing most people think of when they hear about mindfulness is seated meditation—which is by far the most discussed and studied tool for mindfulness. But the point of seated meditation isn't just to spend 5, 15, or 30 minutes of your day settling down and practicing mindfulness. The point of formal practice is to be able to bring those feelings with you as you move through your days, your relationships, your job and your community.

There are many different meditation styles and techniques, from mantra to mindfulness to sensory ... and the list goes on. One of the most frequently asked questions I get is about the difference between the many styles, techniques, and programs—so I put together this overview of some popular types of seated meditation.

This is by no means meant to be a comprehensive guide to the many different forms, subdivisions, lineages, and meditations that are out there, just an overview of some of the most popular. Some of the styles I'll discuss are more traditional, others are Western styles or meditation programs that were inspired from the more traditional teachings, some overlap, and all are beneficial.

Remember—there is no best form of meditation—the best style is the one you will actually practice with consistency. So try a few out and see what feels best for you.

Mindfulness Meditation

Mindfulness meditation is the umbrella term for the category of techniques used to create awareness and insight by practicing focused attention, observing, and accepting all that arises without judgment. Although the origins of mindfulness meditation come from Buddhist teachings—predominantly *Vipassana* meditation, but also incorporates philosophies and practices from other Buddhist traditions—the style and way it's taught is nonsectarian and appeals to people from many different religions and cultures. Its simple nature and open philosophy has made it the most popular meditation technique in the West.

- **Who should try mindfulness meditation?** It's a great practice for anyone getting started in meditation or wanting to dive deeper into their practice; Especially suitable for beginners who don't have access to a teacher, as the instructions are simple and there are many free and accessible resources and guided meditations on the Internet.

- **Well-known mindfulness teachers**: Jon-Kabat Zinn, Tara Brach, Sharon Salzberg, Joseph Goldestein, Jack Kornfield, Pema Chodron

Mindfulness-Based Stress Reduction

Mindfulness-Based Stress Reduction, or MBSR, is an eight-week program that integrates mindfulness meditation and yoga with Western medicine and science. Jon Kabat-Zinn developed the program in 1979, drawing from many years as a student of Buddhism and yoga. He integrated these teachings with his background in science and designed a meditation program (although he doesn't call it meditation) that supports Western medicine to help people manage their stress, anxiety, illnesses, and chronic pain. He made the program extremely accessible and attractive to all types of people, and helped the general public understand that you don't need to be a Buddhist to practice meditation. You can find MBSR courses offered at medical centers, universities, hospitals, and clinics around the world.

- **Who should try MBSR?** Anyone suffering from chronic pain, illness or anxiety; Anyone curious about meditation but skeptical about spirituality; People who like evidence and data to support activity; Rookie meditators who want a supportive community to start their practice

- **Creator**: Jon-Kabat Zinn

*Learn more about MBSR and my experience in the course: at http://mindfulminutes.com/mbsr/

Primordial Sound Meditation

Primordial Sound Meditation, or PSM for short, is a mantra-based meditation technique rooted in the Vedic tradition of India. Deepak Chopra and David Simon revived this ancient practice at the Chopra Center for Wellbeing, and created a mantra-based meditation program anyone can practice. In PSM, each individual is given a mantra based on the vibration the universe was creating at the time and location of their birth. The mantra is used as a tool to take your mind to a quieter place. During meditation, you silently repeat the mantra, which creates a vibration that helps you slip into a place below the noisy chatter of the mind, and into stillness and pure awareness.

- **Who should try PSM?** Spiritually-minded individuals; People looking for structure in their meditation practice; Those new to meditation and serious about incorporating it into their lives

- **Creator**: Deepak Chopra

Vipassana Meditation

Vipassana is often known as insight meditation, translated to mean, "to see things as they really are." Also a traditional Buddhist meditation practice, *Vipassana* emphasizes awareness of the breath, tuning into the air passing in and out through the nose. *Vipassana* also teaches you to label thoughts and experiences as they arise, taking mental notes as you identify objects that grab your attention. Each time you identify a label in your mind, you are then encouraged to bring your awareness back to your primary object, being the breath. There are several different types of *Vipassana* meditation that have evolved from the traditional style over the years.

- **Who should try** *Vipassana*? Excellent for beginners; People looking to practice meditation in an entirely secular context or combined with another religion or belief system; Those interested in trying a silent retreat

- **Well-known** *Vipassana* **teachers**: Sharon Salzberg, Joseph Goldestein, Jack Kornfield, Michael Stone

*Vipassana is also known for it's silent retreats, offered around the world as a way to dive deeper into meditation practice and the inner world.

Zen Meditation (*Zazen*)

Zazen means "seated meditation" in Japanese. Most people know the meditation practice as simply Zen meditation, a type of Buddhist meditation where you focus your awareness on your breath and observe thoughts and experiences as they pass through the mind and environment, letting them float by. This may sound remarkably similar to *Vipassana* meditation, and that's because it is similar. Although there are some differences, most would seem far more apparent to experienced meditators than those just starting out. One main practical difference is that in Zen meditation, the emphasis of the breath is at the belly, instead of the nose (as in *Vipassana*). Another big difference is that posture is much stricter in Zen meditation than in *Vipassana*, with stringent attention on a straight spine, tucked chin, and hands placed in a special position over the belly. In Zen, eyes are always instructed to be open, with a downcast gaze, and in *Vipassana*, there are not strict rules for the eye gaze, and beginners are encouraged to keep them closed.

- **Who should try Zen?** Those who already have some experience with meditation; Those who can handle rigid rules for practice and don't mind little instruction; Those who like the idea of practicing with a teacher

- **Well-known Zen teachers**: Thich Nhat Hanh, Joan Halifax Roshi, Adyashanti

Transcendental Meditation

Transcendental Meditation, or TM, is another mantra-based meditation technique. As with PSM, its origin is from Ancient India and each person is given a personal mantra used for its vibrational qualities to help settle the mind. Although the purpose of the meditation and the technique itself is similar to PSM, there are quite a few differences, including the mantras themselves and how they are selected, the instruction of meditation, and the recommended length of time to meditate.

- **Who should try Transcendental Meditation?** People looking for structure in their meditation practice; Those new to meditation and serious about incorporating it into life; Those willing to spend money on their mantra

- **Creator**: Maharishi Mahesh Yogi

Loving-Kindness Meditation

Loving-kindness meditation is also known as Metta meditation, meaning unconditional kindness and friendliness. This meditation style also originates from Buddhist teachings, mainly Tibetan Buddhism. In the growing field of compassion research, the loving-kindness meditation has been proven to be particularly helpful with boosting empathy, positivity, acceptance, and kindness toward oneself and others.

The traditional loving-kindness meditation always starts with sending loving-kindness to oneself, then continues to send it in this order: to a friend or loved one, to someone who is neutral in your life, to a difficult person, and then out to the universe.

- **Who should try Loving-Kindness meditation?** Anyone with low self-esteem, high levels of self-criticism, and a desire to grow more empathetic with others

- **Well-known instructors who teach Loving-Kindness meditation**: Sharon Saltzberg, Pema Chodron

Kundalini Meditation

In Kundalini meditation, the main idea is that through meditation, you awaken your untapped Kundalini energy, located at the base of the spine. When this energy is released, it travels up the spine and leads to an experience commonly known as Kunadalini awakening, which ultimately leads to enlightenment. Kundalini meditations can include breathing techniques, mantras, mudras (hand placements), and chants to tap into the power of the unconscious mind and bring it forward to energize and awaken the conscious mind.

- **Who should try Kundalini meditation?** Open-minded individuals; those looking to dive deeper into their spirituality

- **Well-known Kundalini teachers**: Gurmukh Kaur Khalsa; Harijiwan

Yoga Nidra

Yoga Nidra is the Sanskrit phrase for yogic sleep. As the name suggests, it's a restful, deeply relaxing practice, and it originated from the Tantra tradition in yoga. Yoga Nidra is done lying down or in a reclined, comfortable posture, and although this may look like a nap, you are fully conscious during the practice. If you're in a class, teachers will usually recommend props, like blankets and bolsters, so you can find as much comfort and ease in the body as possible.

The meditation itself involves a step-by-step process of visualization and guided instructions that lead you into a deep state of conscious relaxation.

- **Who should try Yoga Nidra?** Anyone, Yoga Nidra is great for releasing stress ... and who doesn't experience stress? It's especially helpful for those who are stressed out but have trouble focusing on just one thing at a time (like mantra or breath-awareness meditations)

- **Well-known yogis who teach Yoga Nidra**: Many teachers who teach asana also offer Yoga Nidra, including Dharma Mittra and Rod Stryker

Chakra Meditations

A chakra is an energetic center in the body, and we have seven of them, each located in a different area of the body and each associated with a different color, sound, and energetic purpose. From the practice of yoga, chakra meditations can be very powerful, especially when focusing on and connecting with one element in the physical or emotional body at a time. Many chakra meditations use sound, specific placement of hands, and visualization techniques to connect with the chakras and bring healing energy to an issue or emotion that needs attention.

- **Who should try chakra meditations?** Chakra meditations are a great compliment to those already practicing yoga; Those looking to heal something in their physical or energetic bodies; Spiritually-minded individuals

Tonglen Meditation

Tonglen meditation is a Tibetan Buddhist meditation that is meant to connect you with suffering in an effort to help you overcome it. In the West, we are often taught to avoid suffering, sometimes through seeking pleasure, which is the exact opposite of how Tonglen teaches you to manage suffering and challenge. In these meditations, you develop an attitude of openness toward suffering, let go of negativity, practice giving and receiving, and cultivate compassion and empathy through the breath, visualization, and intention—for ourselves and others. The practice can be done in any comfortable position, whether seated or reclined.

- **Who should try Tonglen meditation?** Anyone dealing with difficult people, stress and/or negativity; Those struggling with self-criticism and self-doubt; Those who want to cultivate compassion and kindness toward themselves and others; Those seeking spiritual growth

- **Well-known leaders who teach Tonglen meditation**: Pema Chodron, His Holiness the Dalai Lama

Glossary of Zazen & Buddhist Terms

Abhidhamma/Abhidharma (Pali/Sanskrit)

The third section of the Buddhist canon devoted to human psychology and philosophy

Anapanasati (Pali)

Mindfulness of breathing

Anatta (Pali)

Not self, insubstantiality, one of the three characteristics of existence

Anicca (Pali)

Impermanent, one of the three characteristics of existence. Buddhist teachings emphasize that all conditioned mental and physical phenomena are impermanent — nothing lasts, nothing stays the same.

Arahant (Pali)

Enlightened one; someone whose mind is completely free from the defilements; a person who is no longer bound to cyclic existence

Beginner's mind

A mind that is open to the experience of the moment, free of conceptual overlays; first made popular by the Zen teacher Suzuki Roshi

Bhikkhu (Pali)

A Buddhist monk

Bhikkhuni (Pali)

A Buddhist nun

Bodhi (Pali/Sanskrit)

Enlightenment, awakening

Bodhicitta (Sanskrit)

Wisdom-heart or the awakened heart/mind; the aspiration for supreme enlightenment so that all sentient beings may be free from suffering

Bodhisatta/Bodhisattva (Pali/Sanskrit)

One who has taken a vow to become a fully enlightened Buddha; someone known for an unbounded readiness and availability to help all sentient beings

Bodhi tree

The tree under which the Buddha attained enlightenment in Bodh Gaya, India — a fig tree popularly called Pipal (*Ficus Religiosa*)

Brahma-Vihara (Pali, Sanskrit)

Heavenly or sublime abode, the four mind states said to lead to a rebirth in a heavenly realm: lovingkindness (*metta*), compassion (*karuna*), appreciative joy (*mudita*) and equanimity (*upekkha*)

Buddha (Pali, Sanskrit)

Fully awakened one; specifically the historical Buddha, Sakyamuni, who lived and taught in India 2,500 years ago; one of the three jewels of refuge

Buddha-Dharma/Dhamma (Sanskrit/Pali)

The teachings of the Buddha

Dana (Pali/Sanskrit)

The practice of giving; generosity. Dana is the first of the ten paramis, or qualities to be perfected in order to become a Buddha

Dhammapada (Pali)

The best known of all the Buddhist scriptures; a collection of 423 verses, spoken by the Buddha, that focuses on the value of ethical conduct and mental training

Dependent origination

The doctrine that all mental and physical phenomena arise and pass away depending on causes and conditions

Dharma/Dhamma (Sanskrit/Pali)

The Buddha's teachings, truth, the basic building blocks of reality; one of the three jewels of refuge

Dukkha (Pali)

Suffering; of pain, both mental and physical, of change, and endemic to cyclic existence; the first Noble Truth that acknowledges the reality of suffering

Ego

The pattern of conditioned habits that we mistake for a sense of self

Enlightenment

Awakening

Feeling tone

Vedana (Pali); the pleasant, unpleasant or neutral tone that arises with every experience; one of the five aggregates

Investigation

Vicaya (Pali); Interest and inquiry into experience. One of the seven factors of enlightenment

Jhana (Pali)

Mental absorption, a state of strong concentration that temporarily suspends the five hindrances

Joy

Piti (Pali); A gladdening of the mind and body. One of the seven factors of enlightenment

Kalyana mitta (Pali)

Spiritual friend. In the Theravada Buddhist meditation tradition, teachers are often referred to as spiritual friends.

Karma/Kamma (Sanskrit/Pali)

Action, deed; the law of cause and effect; intentional action, either wholesome or unwholesome that brings either pleasant or unpleasant results respectively

Kilesa (Pali)

Defilement; unwholesome qualities; a factor of mind that obscures clear seeing; a hindrance to meditation; also know as afflictive emotion

Karuna (Pali)

Compassion; one of the four Brahma-Viharas (sublime abodes)

Mental noting

A technique used in meditation to help direct the mind to the object of meditation

Merit

The auspicious power of wholesome action that brings positive karmic results

Metta (Pali)

Loving kindness, gentle friendship; a practice for generating lovingkindness said to be first taught by the Buddha as an antidote to fear. It helps cultivate our natural capacity for an open and loving heart and is traditionally offered along with other Brahma-vihara meditations that enrich compassion, joy in the happiness of others and equanimity. These practices lead to the development of concentration, fearlessness, happiness and a greater ability to love.

Middle way

A spiritual path that avoids extremes of self-mortification and self-indulgence, as discovered and taught by the Buddha

Mindfulness

Sati (Pali). Careful attention to mental and physical processes; a key ingredient of meditation; one of the five spiritual faculties; one of the seven factors of enlightenment; an aspect of the Noble Eightfold Path

Mudita (Pali)

Appreciative or empathetic joy; the cultivation of happiness when seeing someone else's good fortune or happy circumstances; one of the four Brahma-Viharas (sublime abodes)

Neutral person

In the context of metta (lovingkindness) practice, someone for whom you feel no particular liking or disliking

Nirvana/ Nibbana (Sanskrit/Pali)

Extinction of the fires of attachment, hatred and delusion that cause suffering; liberation from cyclic existence

Pali

The ancient language of the scriptures of Theravada Buddhism

Panna (Pali)

Wisdom; one of the five spiritual faculties

Parami (Pali)

The qualities of character to be perfected in order to become a Buddha. The ten paramis are...

Precept

A principle that defines a certain standard of ethical conduct; the foundation of all Buddhist meditation practice; see the five (or eight) precepts

Restlessness and remorse

Uddhacca-kukkucca (Pali). Agitation of the mind; one of the five hindrances to meditation

Saddha (Pali)

Faith, confidence; one of the five spiritual faculties

Samadhi (Pali)

Concentration; a deep state of meditation; one of the five spiritual faculties; one of the seven factors of enlightenment; an aspect of the Noble Eightfold Path

Samatha (Pali)

A term referring to the group of meditation practices that aim at samadhi

Samsara (Pali, Sanskrit)

Wandering on; round of rebirths; the ocean of worldly suffering; the state of being governed by the five hindrances

Sangha (Pali)

The community of practitioners of the Buddhist path, or those beings who have attained direct realization of the nature of reality, one of the three jewels of refuge.

Sankhara (Pali)

Mental or physical formation

Sati (Pali)

Mindfulness; one of the five spiritual faculties; of the seven factors of enlightenment; an aspect of the Noble Eightfold Path

Satipatthana (Pali)

The four foundations of mindfulness: contemplation of body, feeling, mind and mind-objects; the Buddha's quintessential teachings on mindfulness

Sense doors

The six perceptual gates through which we experience the world. The six sense doors are...

Sila (Pali)

Moral or ethical conduct, virtue, the foundation of Buddhist practice

Skeptical doubt

Vicikiccha (Pali). The kind of doubt that undermines faith; one of the five hindrances to meditation

Skillful means

Action based on kindness, respect, truthfulness, timeliness and wisdom

Sloth and torpor

Thina-middha (Pali) Sleepiness; one of the five hindrances to meditation

Sutta/Sutra (Pali/Sanskrit)

Thread, heard; a discourse by the Buddha or one of his disciples

Theravada (Pali)

Path of the Elders; the form of Buddhism found throughout many parts of Southeast Asia. Vipassana meditation is a central part of this tradition.

Three jewels of refuge

The three jewels of refuge are the Buddha, the Dharma (doctrine) and the Sangha. Practitioners take refuge in the fact that the Buddha found a way to freedom, taught the Dharma as the path to that freedom, and founded the Sangha as the supportive community that follows the way.

Tranquility

Passaddhi (Pali); Physical and mental calm. One of the seven factors of enlightenment

Upekkha (Pali)

Equanimity; the ability to maintain a spacious impartiality of mind in the midst of life's changing conditions; one of the four Brahma-Viharas (sublime abodes); one of the seven factors of enlightenment

Vedana (Pali)

Feeling; the pleasant, unpleasant or neutral feeling tone that arises with all experience; one of the five aggregates

Vinaya (Pali)

Discipline; the rules and regulations governing the conduct of Buddhist monks and nuns

Vipassana (Pali)

To see clearly; insight meditation; the simple and direct practice of moment-to-moment mindfulness. Through careful and sustained observation, we experience for ourselves the ever-changing flow of the mind/body process. This awareness leads us to accept more fully the pleasure and pain, fear and joy, sadness and happiness that life inevitably brings. As insight deepens, we develop greater equanimity and peace in the face of change, and wisdom and compassion increasingly become the guiding principles of our lives.

The Buddha first taught vipassana over 2,500 years ago. The various methods of this practice have been well preserved in the Theravada tradition of Buddhism. IMS retreats are all rooted in this ancient and well-mapped path to awakening and draw on the full spectrum of this tradition's lineages.

Viriya (Pali)

The physical and mental energy needed for diligent mindfulness practice; the strong, courageous heart of energy. One of the five spiritual faculties; one of the seven factors of enlightenment

Wrong view

The tendency of the mind to cling to concepts at the expense of reality; taking what is impermanent to be permanent, what is dissatisfying to be satisfying, what is selfless to be self

Yogi (Pali)

One who is undertaking the spiritual path of awakening; a meditator

The three characteristics

The three characteristics of all conditioned physical and mental phenomena:

1. Impermanent; *anicca* (Pali)
2. Unsatisfactory, suffering; *dukkha* (Pali)
3. Non-self; *anatta* (Pali)

The three feeling tones

Each moment of experience is felt as one of three feeling tones:

1. Pleasant
2. Unpleasant
3. Neutral; neither pleasant nor unpleasant

The three kinds of suffering

The Buddha taught that we can understand different kinds of suffering through these three categories:

1. The suffering of mental and physical pain
2. The suffering of change
3. The suffering of conditionality

The four Brahma-Viharas

These four 'sublime abodes' reflect the mind state of enlightenment:

1. Lovingkindness; *metta* (Pali)
2. Compassion; *karuna* (Pali)
3. Appreciative joy; *mudita* (Pali)
4. Equanimity; *upekkha* (Pali)

The four foundations of mindfulness

The Buddha's quintessential teachings on mindfulness:

1. Contemplation of body
2. Contemplation of feeling
3. Contemplation of mind
4. Contemplation of mind-objects

The four noble truths

This was the Buddha's first and fundamental teaching about the nature of our experience and our spiritual potential:

1. The existence of suffering
2. The origin of suffering
3. The cessation of suffering
4. The path to the cessation of suffering — the Noble Eightfold Path

The five aggregates of clinging

The five aspects of personality in which all physical and mental phenomena exist:

1. Materiality; *rupa* (Pali)
2. Feeling; *vedana* (Pali)
3. Perception; *sanna* (Pali)
4. Mental formations; *sankhara* (Pali)
5. Consciousness; *vinnana* (Pali)

The five hindrances

These are the classical hindrances to meditation practice:

1. Desire, clinging, craving; *kamacchanda* (Pali)

2. Aversion, anger, hatred; *vyapada* (Pali)

3. Sleepiness, sloth, torpor; *thina-midha* (Pali)

4. Restlessness and remorse; *uddhacca-kukkucca* (Pali)

5. Skeptical doubt; *vicikiccha* (Pali)

The five (or eight) precepts

An ethical life is founded on these standards of conduct:

1. To practice compassionate action – to refrain from harming any living, sentient beings.

2. To practice contentment – to refrain from taking what is not freely given. To not steal or 'borrow' without the consent of the giver; to accept what is offered and not try to change it or get more.

3. To practice responsibility in all our relationships – including refraining from misusing sexual energy. (While on retreat, yogis take the precept to abstain from sexual activity.)

4. To refrain from harmful speech – not to lie, gossip or use harsh or hurtful language.

5. To care for ourselves – to refrain from clouding the mind and harming the body through the misuse of alcohol, drugs and other intoxicants.

During most IMS retreats offered by monastic teachers, retreatants are asked to abide by the eight precepts. The additional three precepts are:

6. To refrain from eating after noon.

7. To refrain from dancing, singing, music, shows; from the use of garlands, perfumes,

8. cosmetics and adornments.
9. To refrain from using high and luxurious seats and beds.

The five spiritual faculties

These are inherent faculties of mind and heart that, when fully developed, lead to the end of suffering:

1. Faith; *saddha* (Pali)
2. Energy; *viriya* (Pali)
3. Mindfulness; *sati* (Pali)
4. Concentration; *samadhi* (Pali)
5. Wisdom; *panna* (Pali)

The six sense doors

Everything we experience comes through these portals:

1. Eye (Seeing)
2. Ear (Hearing)
3. Nose (Smelling)
4. Tongue (Tasting)
5. Body (Touching)
6. Mind

The six wholesome and unwholesome roots of mind

The mind is always under the influence of one of these states:

Wholesome

1. Generosity; *dana* (Pali)
2. Lovingkindness; *metta* (Pali)
3. Wisdom; *panna* (Pali)

Unwholesome

1. Greed; *lobha* (Pali)
2. Hatred; *dosa* (Pali)
3. Delusion; *moha* (Pali)

The seven factors of enlightenment

The mental qualities that provide the conditions conducive to awakening:

1. Mindfulness; *sati* (Pali)
2. Investigation; *vicaya* (Pali)
3. Energy; *viriya* (Pali)
4. Joy; *piti* (Pali)
5. Tranquility; *passaddhi* (Pali)
6. Concentration; *samadhi* (Pali)
7. Equanimity; *upekkha* (Pali)

The noble eightfold path

This is the path the Buddha taught to those seeking liberation:

1. Right view
2. Right thought
3. Right speech
4. Right action
5. Right livelihood
6. Right effort
7. Right mindfulness
8. Right concentration

The eight worldly vicissitudes

According to the Buddha, we will experience these vicissitudes throughout lives, no matter what our intentions or actions:

1. Gain and loss
2. Praise and blame
3. Pleasure and pain
4. Fame and disrepute

The ten paramis

These are the qualities of character that, when perfected, lead to Buddhahood:

1. Generosity
2. Morality
3. Renunciation
4. Wisdom

5. Energy
6. Patience
7. Truthfulness
8. Resoluteness
9. Lovingkindness
10. Equanimity

www.ingramcontent.com/pod-product-compliance
Lightning Source LLC
Chambersburg PA
CBHW071731090426
42738CB00011B/2458